Thai Ridgeback

A Complete Thai Ridgeback Pet Owner's Guide

Thai Ridgeback Dog Basics, Choosing and Owning, Breeding, Care, Feeding, Grooming and Training All Included!

By: Lolly Brown

Foreword

Welcome! You're about to make a truly wonderful a life-changing journey if you decide to get yourself a Thai Ridgeback dog!

If you're considering getting a Thai Ridgeback dog to be a part of your family, loving him and then receiving unconditional love in return, you are making a momentous decision.

What's inside this book?

Included inside this book's first section is about the origin and bio of a Thai Ridgeback dog. It contains the general information and the characteristics of this specific dog breed.

The Second section is about choosing a Thai Ridgeback dog. It tackles about where and how to acquire a Thai Ridgeback and how to get your paperwork done.

The next section will talk about the things that you need and have to do as a Thai Ridgeback dog owner.

The fourth section focuses on how you can cater your Thai Ridgeback dog's nutritional needs.

The next section delves into basic care and regular grooming needs for your Thai Ridgeback dog.

The sixth section is about raising and training your Thai Ridgeback dog. It educates dog owners about the importance of training and activities for your dog. It additionally contains a puppy's training outline and guidance in shaping behaviors, training, and problem solving.

Th seventh section focuses on the common health issues of and how to deal with them and respond into emergencies.

For the last section, it will talk about the breeding process for your Thai Ridgeback dog.

By obtaining this training guide, you will be on your way to securing the necessary tools and knowledge to assure your success as a Thai Ridgeback dog owner and trainer.

Table of Contents

Introduction

A Thai Ridgeback puppy requires a healthy upbringing from the beginning. All puppies will have certain bad tendencies that you will need to break and train into good ones. They need to be well taken care of and fed, but part of that care also includes receiving quality education from a young age.

As a Thai Ridgeback dog owner, there are many things to work through and plan for, and there will be unexpected situations that need thoughtful resolution. Through it all, it will be important to remember that you are embarking on a journey of team togetherness with your puppy. Take everything one step at a time, day by day. Don't become bogged down by challenges, and relish every joyful, fun-filled moment.

There will be tests and trials, but stick to your goals each and every day. Take comfort in the fact that puppyhood passes quickly and it won't be long before your hard work pays off as your pup grows up to be a reliable and well-trained adult dog who is a pleasure to live with.

As soon as you start raising your Thai Ridgeback puppy, you will have a clear understanding of how to train and understand your pet. In time, you will be able to proudly and confidently take your furry friend with you anywhere you go. Additionally, you will establish a strong friendship system with your pet for years to come.

I will show you how you can have a well-behaved, healthy, and happy Thai Ridgeback dog.

Let's start our journey!

Chapter One: Thai Ridgeback Facts and Descriptions

Origin

The Thai Ridgeback used to be first documented roughly 350 years ago, but breed fans trust that the breed has existed naturally for an awful lot longer than that. Humans in Thailand semi-domesticated the breed in the 1600s for more than one purpose: to chase down vermin, assist pull carts, and act as a defend for retail outlets and homes. Before (and even after) domestication, Thai Ridgebacks had been typically discovered on the jap island of Dao PhuQuoc, proper close to the border of Cambodia and Vietnam.

The breed is nonetheless fantastically uncommon outdoor in Thailand, and many golf equipment backyard of Thailand no longer formally understand the primitive breed. The Thai Ridgeback did not even make it over to the States till 1994. The American Kennel Club introduced the Thai Ridgeback to their Foundational Stock Service crew in 1997.

Physical Characteristics

This breed has a short, smooth coat with pricked ears. It gained its name from the ridge of hair that runs down the dog's back.

Size

A Thai Ridgeback is a medium-sized, muscular, pariah-type dog. Male Thai Ridgebacks stand 22 to 24 inches from the shoulder and weigh between 50 and 70 pounds, whilst female lady Thai Ridgebacks stand a little shorter at 20 to 22 inches and weigh around 35 to 55 pounds.

Still, some Thai Ridgebacks can be large or smaller than common for their breed.

Coat Color

The coat of a Thai Ridgeback is smooth, short and coat comes in a variety of colors, namely black, red, blue, and light fawn.

Temperament

The Thai Ridgeback—originally bred as a hunting partner and watchdog—is a quick-witted breed. Because of their historic guarding duties, the pups are incredibly affectionate and loyal companions to family members they trust.

Due to the Thai Ridgeback's innate ability to guard and hunt without proper training, it might turn out to be overprotective of you and become somewhat aggressive towards strangers.

Lifespan

The life expectancy of a Thai Ridgeback ranges between 12–13 years.

Chapter Two: Choosing and Acquiring a Thai Ridgeback

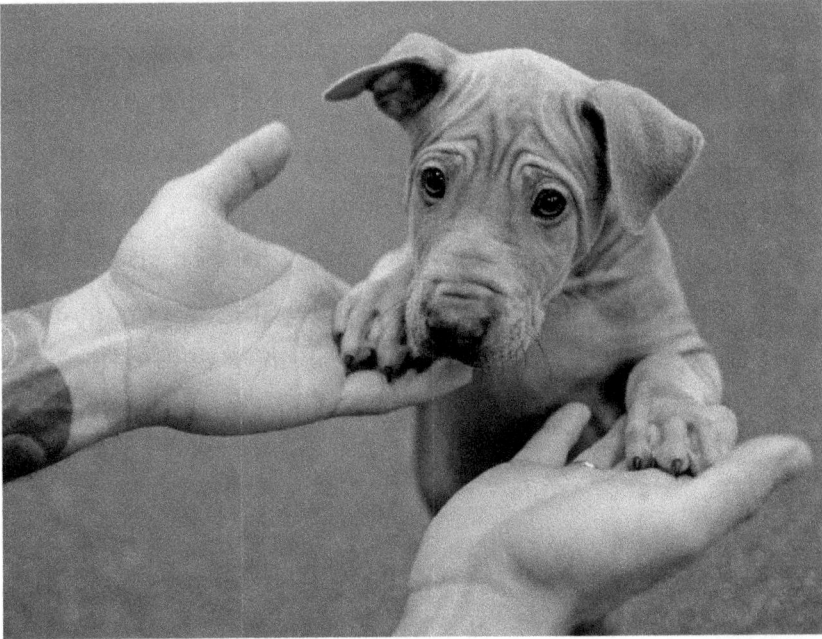

Where To Acquire Your Thai Ridgeback

There are so many places you can buy a Thai Ridgeback dog in the market. Here are some of them;

Find A Reputable Breeder

When you are buying a specific pure breed, this is the best way to go. You must find not only a responsible breeder but also one that is ethical. This means that you do your homework well to ensure that you don't settle for a breeder who does not practice ethical breeding.

The trick is to ask your veterinarian and other dog owners to give you more information on responsible breeders in the areas. To get a list of reputable breeders, you can visit the American Kennel Club website. To know a responsible and ethical breeder, they will be happy to take you around their breeding facility and answer all the questions you might have. They will also have documentation of their veterinary care and will give you a health guarantee and contract.

Animal Shelters And Rescue Groups

If you buying a Thai Ridgeback dog through a breeder is out of your budget, the next option you might want to look at is a local animal shelter or rescue group. It is also important that you work with a veterinarian to point in the right rescue groups or reputable animal shelters.

Alternatively, you can do a simple online search of the animal shelters within your areas. For instance, the Shelter Pet project, adopt a pet, and Petfinder, just to mention but a few. The good thing with this option is that the cost of adopting a dog is low. You can simply visit their websites to find out their adoptable dogs and learn more about them.

Note that animal shelters have several mixed-breeds with fewer health issues. If you are looking for an adult dog, this is the best way to go.

Visiting Local Animal Shelters

It is important to note that rescue groups tend to foster care dogs. If you are not sure whether to buy a Thai Ridgeback dog and if they will suit your lifestyle, you can simply foster a dog. Visiting a local animal shelter within your area will offer you a good chance of seeing the dogs in person and determining whether you are comfortable with their way of caring for dogs.

That said, note that visiting an animal shelter can be an emotional experience. Ensure that you can keep your emotions in check. The best way is to bring a notepad with you to take notes as you see the dogs.

You will realize that most animal shelters have moved away from same-day adoptions just to ensure that people don't impulse adopt. Therefore, when you go into an animal share, bear in mind that you will not go home with a dog that day. Get ready for several visits and long application processes to ensure that you want a dog, and the one you get is the right fit for you.

During your visits to the animal shelter, ensure that you ask as many questions as you can – for the Thai Ridgeback you are interested in getting. Find out about their lineage, medical history, behavioral assessment, and veterinary care. Ask questions about their shelter, types of food, and their nutritional value. This way, you can continue their feeding program when you adopt them before you can slowly transition them to new foods. Find out about their adoption fees per breed.

Don't Buy A Dog From A Pet Store Or On The Internet

Well, we cannot emphasize this enough – buying a dog in a pet store directly online is a bad idea! If you are in the market for a dog, the last place you want to look at is the pet store. These dogs often come from puppy mills that keep dogs under deplorable conditions. These dogs also suffer serious behavioral and health problems.

You must note that buying a dog is not like getting your favorite clothes from Amazon or other sites online. You have to see what you are buying so that you can decide whether it is the right fit. Plus, shipping a dog long distance risks them suffering serious physical and emotional stress.

Getting The Paperwork Done

Where are you buying your Thai Ridgeback dog from? This is one of the most important factors in ensuring that you have your paperwork right. If you are acquiring the Thai Ridgeback puppy from a breeder, you must have an agreement/contract in writing. Trust me, even though you know the dealer personally, it is important that you have everything spelled out in writing. You may not know what the other party expects from you until you have everything on paper.

Ensure that you thoroughly and carefully read through the contract that your breeder gives you before you sign on the dotted line. Don't sign the contract before you complete the purchase. Often, breeder's contracts will stipulate that the dog be spayed and that if you ever need to give them up, you must return it to them. In other words, buying a pup from a breeder is very expensive and comes with several requirements that you must fully understand before you commit.

The truth is, what belongs in the contract will often depend on why you are buying the dog in the first place. If you are buying a purebred registered with AKC, that information is something you want to be captured in the contract. If you just want to own a healthy mixed-breed, then you don't need to worry about having that pedigree in the agreement. If adopting one from an animal shelter, you are not really buying. Even so, you still need to have all the answers about the puppy captured in the paperwork.

Your contract should have the following information;

Health status

Has a vet examined them? If you find out that your pooch is sick, can you return it or be reimbursed for the vet bills? If they have a serious condition within a couple of weeks of buying, can you take it back?

Vaccination information

What vaccinations have the dog received so far? What other vaccinations do they need, and when should they have them? Which veterinarian of the clinic did they receive the vaccinations, the dates, and all documentations? This way, you have everything when you need a license.

Dog history

Where did they come from? What about its lineage?

Training

Has it been trained? Is there proof of training in terms of documentation on the training and the durations they took?

Quality

Is it a purebred or a mixed breed?

Price

Does the price include all vaccinations? What about the cost of spaying or neutering?

Warranty?

Does the seller offer warranties? What kinds of warranties do you get for buying one?

You also must have proof of ownership in case you ever have to show for it.

It is important that you get a recent picture of your cute Thai Ridgeback puppy, and whether you consider them a part of your family or property? This can be as simple as the adoption records and the AKC registration records as well. Also, ensure that you fill out a pet agreement form that shows who is responsible for ownership and pet care. This is especially important if the dog is acquired by two people who are not married.

One last word

Indeed, buying a dog, where to buy and how to buy, is the most important information you need to know when considering an addition to the family. One thing you must bear in mind is that getting a pooch will change your life for the better. There are so many new things you will need to learn to ensure that you start the adventure the right way and in the right direction.

Before you walk into a breeder's facility, animal shelter, or rescue group, you must ask yourself whether you are truly ready to own a pup. Realize that this is a huge responsibility that calls for time, effort, and commitment – financially, emotionally, and physically. You must be certain and ready before you can bring a bundle of love into your life.

What type of breed are you interested in owning? Is Thai Ridgeback the right one for you? Some of the factors that will ensure that you choose the right breed for you include size, age, activity level, and budget. All these are defined by the lifestyle and personal preferences you might have. It is also important that you put into perspective their personality traits, their health concerns, grooming needs, and ease of training.

Finally, where do you intend to get your cuddly from? A breeder, rescue group or animal shelters are some of the best places to get a healthy dog from. However, there are certain places you must beware when looking for a puppy – such as online, pet shops, and flea markets. These places risk you losing your money or getting a puppy that has problems all around. Buying from these places is simply choosing to keep irresponsible and unethical people in the business. Unless you know that a dog you are buying or adopting is legitimate, don't buy.

That said, if you put into consideration all the information we have discussed here, you are on your way to owning a healthy Thai Ridgeback puppy and having so much fun taking care of each other.

Chapter Three: Preparing for Your Thai Ridgeback

At last, the Thai Ridgeback puppy you've wanted for so long is finally home. This is an exciting time for you; but for your pet, it can be a very stressful adjustment. Your new puppy will be leaving the security of their mother and littermates. They will be experiencing new sights, sounds, and smells - unfamiliar ones at that. In order to prepare for this transition, here are a couple of tips you need to do in order to get your puppy settled in your new home.

Essential Supplies

Stainless steel bowls for food and water

Provide durable bowls for your teething puppies as these can withstand rust, breakages or chips. Puppies will naturally bite and chew anything in sight, which can be a big problem when using plastic bowls. Plus, stainless bowls are more sanitary. Find a permanent place for these food bowls so that the puppy develops the familiar routine of going to where the food and water are when he needs them.

Sleeping place

Giving your Thai Ridgeback puppy his own safe place to sleep on is essential in making him feel secure, take refuge and sleep. Provide a comfortable bed or a puppy crate in the corner.

Collar and leash

In order to get your Thai Ridgeback puppy used to wearing a leash and collar, you need to start using them right away. Make sure that the collar is snug enough not to slip over his head, but not too tight. You can also provide a dog tag for identification.

Brush and comb

You want your Thai Ridgeback puppy to grow up being familiar with handling by different people, and grooming is the easiest way to do that. It can also make brushing and combing easier for both of you as your puppy grows bigger and stronger. This will also save you a lot of hassle when your dear one goes to the vet for general checkups or vaccinations.

Puppy toys

Choose a toy that is very durable. Purchase rubber toys that are smaller than your puppies for teething purposes, and larger size ones for larger puppies. Choose only safe toys, and discard or throw out the ones that already show signs of wear and tear. In order to encourage them to play with their toys, you should set aside some playtime to get your puppy's attention – and this will also function as invaluable bonding time. Playtime can be used as an alternative to food treats as it is also a valuable reward. Remember, puppies want nothing more than to spend as much time as they can with their master, so this can function as positive reinforcement.

Treats

Just like humans, dogs are social creatures. To facilitate bonding between you and your furry friend, keep treats in handy. These are an effective and appropriate training tool and a great way to say, "Well-done," in terms your dog clearly understands.

Stain and odor remover

Thai Ridgeback dogs can leave stains and odors they may not know about and this is an inevitable part of living with them. There are a variety of effective cleaning products that help you deal with this. Know which ones work for you and remember to choose the ones that are specifically formulated for the use of pets. Using these after a puppy has done his business in the wrong area will erase the scent and lessen the likelihood of a repeat occurrence.

Other optional items include:

✓ ID tag

✓ Crate

✓ Dog shampoo

✓ Puppy/Dog training pads

✓ Clippers

✓ Dog flea treatment

✓ Kennels for outdoor use

✓ Pet gates for indoors

✓ Muzzles

✓   Grooming products and accessories

Preparing Your Home: Dog-Proofing

Just a quick reminder for you: When you get a Thai Ridgeback dog, you're inviting another species into your home. Your dog has no idea how to live in your very human world. The cool thing is that dogs are very adaptable and trainable if you take the time to teach them what they need to do (and not do). By default, dogs will act like, well, dogs. This potentially can include peeing on your expensive carpet, lying all over your comfy couch, and maybe even take a few bites out of your designer shoes. To make sure none of that happens, you have to prepare your home so you can set your new furry friend up to succeed.

Clear the Way

Before you "release the hounds!" in your house, you need to make sure you do a little puppy-proofing. It's not just for young pups, either. Remove any and all objects that will likely tempt your new dog. I recommend looking at your living spaces through the eyes of a dog. Yep, that means getting on your hands and knees and eyeballing everything from a dog's perspective. Look at lower shelves to see if there are any objects that would accessible to him and be aware of spaces he might get into. Things look very different from our perspective, so if you don't get down to your Thai Ridgeback dog's eye level, you might miss some stuff that could be potentially dangerous to him. Plus, you will save your valuables from teeth marks and destruction.

Keep in mind that removing everything is a smart way to start off, but if you want your dog to live in a world that includes shoes, plants, and that ugly rug your mother-in-law got you, you'll need to work with your dog around those items when you can supervise him closely. In the beginning, though, it's best to start with as few distractions as you can manage. Slowly bring your household items back in a controlled setting once you've had some time to build your relationship and get your dog acclimated to his new home.

Remove Choking Hazards

Dogs are like babies when it comes to exploring their world—everything is going to go into their mouth. This is further amplified in dogs because they don't have hands, so they lead with their mouth. This is normal and to be expected, but it can be dangerous. It's very important that you remove anything small enough for your Thai Ridgeback dog to swallow. That also includes anything that they could feasibly bite into pieces. There's nothing worse than an expensive and scary visit to the veterinarian to get an object removed from inside your dog's stomach.

As a general rule, assume your Thai Ridgeback will try to eat it, whatever it is. This is definitely a better-safe-than-sorry approach, so don't gloss over it. Make sure you do an initial sweep of your house, then regularly look it over to make sure nothing is missed. Check small spaces, like the gap between your bed and your nightstand—curious puppies and small dogs can often squeeze into areas that would seem to be too tiny to accommodate a dog. As your Thai Ridgeback learns how to live among all of this interesting human stuff without sampling it, he will build the habit of leaving it all alone and you can relax and be less vigilant.

Relocate or Store Your Valuables

In addition to assessing and removing all of the small objects around your home, it's also a good idea to temporarily remove some of your furniture and any sentimental and expensive items that you want to protect. I don't mean to give you the impression that your new dog is going to come into your house like a wrecking ball, laying waste to everything in his path. Every dog is so different, and some will be well-mannered and respectful of all your stuff right out of the gate. But others can be pretty destructive, and I just want to make sure you're prepared for whatever may happen. I wouldn't want you to start off your relationship with your new dog feeling angry and resentful of him because he made some early mistakes at the expense of your new living room furniture.

So, look around your house for anything that you would be really be upset over if it was damaged. Those items should be removed temporarily until your Thai Ridgeback has acclimated and you feel you can trust him. Area rugs that you like should be rolled up and put in storage, favorite chairs moved to other rooms of the house that will be off-limits to your dog, and any antiques or furniture with sentimental value put out of sight. This is especially important with puppies since they are pretty much guaranteed to have accidents on the floor and will try to chew on everything.

Ditch the Dangers

In addition to removing everything that you value, you also need to make sure there is nothing accessible that could be harmful to your Thai Ridgeback if he were to get ahold of it. Believe it or not, many common items that you love and use without any problems can be very harmful to your dog. It's important to know exactly what these items are and make sure you rearrange your environment so they are out of your dog's reach. You may have to get rid of some things entirely because the risk is just not worth it. Safety first!

Poisons

There are a number of items toxic to Thai Ridgebacks that can be found in every single home, so it's important to note these and make sure your dog stays away from them.

- Pharmaceuticals: Both prescription and over-the-counter medication can be very harmful to your dog and should always be kept out of reach. Even drugs that are prescribed for your Thai Ridgeback by the veterinarian can be dangerous if he consumes a large quantity.

- House plants: Many plants and flowers that you find in and around your house are not safe for dogs. The most common are tulips, sago palm, oleander, philodendrons, rhododendron (also known as azaleas), mistletoe, autumn crocus, and English ivy.

- Essential oils: Essential oils can sometimes be used to help humans and dogs with a number of different ailments. However, others can be harmful if used on or consumed by your dog. Don't assume that just because it's good for you it will have the same effect on your dog. Consult your veterinarian before using any essential oil for your Thai Ridgeback.

- Cleaning supplies: Just about anything you use to clean is not good for your Thai Ridgeback to ingest, so keep all supplies securely stored away.

- Pesticides: If you're treating your lawn or house with any kind of chemical insecticide or fertilizer check to make sure it's pet-safe. If you use a landscaper, be sure to check with them about what they are using on your lawn.

People Food

Although your Thai Ridgeback can get along just fine eating a commercial dog food exclusively, supplementing his diet with whole foods or just surprising him with a special treat every now and then is a great way to put a smile on his face. One thing to keep in mind is that you want to make sure you're rewarding him for good behavior (not begging at the table) and never go from your plate to his bowl. You don't want him to equate your food with his food. Some foods like apples, carrots, bananas, blueberries, and just about any meat (the less seasoned the better) are great for dogs, but there are some foods that are harmful and even potentially life-threatening.

- Chocolate: Chocolate contains theobromine and caffeine and is a big no-no for dogs. I know of a couple of dogs that died after eating it, so be very careful. The most dangerous kinds are baking chocolate and dark chocolate.
- Onions and garlic: These can damage red blood cells and make a dog anemic.

- Grapes and raisins: These are very toxic to your dogs and can cause kidney failure.
- Apple seeds: Apples are good, but the seeds should be removed. If they are chewed by your dog, they can release cyanide (from the natural chemical amygdalin found in apples) when digested.
- Avocados: These contain persin, which can cause vomiting, diarrhea, and heart congestion. That big pit is also a choking hazard.
- Coffee and tea: These can cause vomiting, elevated heart rate and blood pressure, seizures, and even death.
- Macadamia nuts: These are very dangerous for dogs and can cause muscle shakes, vomiting, a rise in temperature, and weakness in the back legs.

Don't Be Shocked

No matter where you live or what kind of a lifestyle you have, we are part of a very plugged-in society. It's great for enjoying the modern conveniences of life, but it poses some potential problems for our dogs. Dogs like to explore their world with their mouths. To your Thai Ridgeback, electrical cords look tasty, feel like a nice chew, and seem like a logical thing to play with, so you need to be very careful.

Chewing up the cords of your electronics will not only get you all steamed up, it can also be dangerous if your Thai

Ridgeback ingests them. A cord may also deliver a jolt of electricity. Supervision is critical to making sure your dog is not tempted by all those cords and for teaching him that they are not there for his enjoyment. Remember, keep your eyes on your dog at all times in the beginning as you learn what kinds of things attract his attention.

Limit Access to Other Rooms

There's a good chance that everything your new Thai Ridgeback is seeing in your house is brand-new and exciting to him. If you've adopted an older dog, you really don't know what he's experienced in his life so far, and if you have a puppy, it's definitely all new to him. When presented with novel stuff, dogs will want to explore, investigate, and sample, which might not be the best thing for you or him. Your job is to supervise him along the way and teach him what things he can interact with and which items in your home are off-limits to him.

The best way to accomplish this is to keep his world small and then slowly expand it as he learns. If you give him too much freedom too quickly, you'll be setting him up to make mistakes. Start small by only giving him access to a couple of rooms and then let him acclimate. When he's doing well, you can expand his environment to include more rooms. Whenever you give him more freedom, make sure you supervise closely to see how he handles the new areas. Keep expanding his world as he shows he's ready—his behavior will dictate how fast you can open things up for him. Depending on how your house is laid out, you can use baby gates and/or closed doors to remove access to certain rooms. Keep in mind that larger dogs and smaller athletic dogs may figure out that they can jump right over the gates if they are motivated enough.

Accidents Will Happen

Even if you've adopted an adult Thai Ridgeback that was described as fully house-trained, you should expect a few accidents as she gets acclimated. Coming into a new home can be stressful, and although your dog may have had a good habit of only going outside before, she doesn't have any history in your house and may get a little confused at first. This is just normal and nothing to worry about. In the beginning, make sure you're taking her out often—even more often than she should be capable of holding it—to give her lots of chances to get it right. This how to start building the repetitions that will shape her habit of only going to the bathroom outside of her new house.

It is a good idea to remove any area rugs or other furniture that you care about for the first month or two. Once your Thai Ridgeback has been doing well and you're confident that's she's developed the habit of going outside, you can bring all your furniture back again.

Securing the Yard

Having a nice fenced-in yard for your Thai Ridgeback to play in is great, but always remember the golden rule: Dogs will act like dogs. Your dog won't just endlessly run laps by himself. He will find something to do and that may include digging holes to the center of the Earth, eating your flowers, and barking at the neighbors—all of which are repetitions and habits that you don't want. So, like with everything else, your dog needs your guidance to teach him how to behave. You need to be outside to reward him for doing the right things and to correct the behaviors you don't like.

Before you get there, though, it's a good idea to take a walk through your yard and scan for anything that might not be safe for your Thai Ridgeback. Walk the entire fence line looking for any gaps at the bottom or holes in the sides that your dog could escape through, including those that you think are too small to be of concern—some dogs are born escape artists! Then look at the objects you have in your yard. Is there anything that he can swallow or chew up? If so, remove them for now. Once your Thai Ridgeback is doing well, you can reintroduce them and see how he does. Finally, check to see what trees, bushes, and plants you have growing back there and make sure none of them are toxic to dogs.

Socializing Your Thai Ridgeback Puppy

There are some dogs that are just born social butterflies, while others need to learn better social skills. Puppy socialization begins with a breeder, and you continue their education in order to keep your puppy confident, happy, and well-adjusted. The breeder should be providing all of their puppies with gentle handling to give the young dogs confidence. They expose them only to positive experiences that include car rides, crates, sounds, smells, and people.

Don't be concerned, but your Thai Ridgeback puppy's first three months of life and their socialization will shape their personality and how they will respond to the environment that surrounds them. Socializing your puppy will accustom them to sounds, smells, and situations that they can handle in a positive way without showing fear.

Socializing After Your Thai Ridgeback Puppy Comes Home

Your breeder got the ball rolling, but after the Thai Ridgeback puppy comes home with you, they are still in a crucial period for learning socialization. It's your job to keep your Thai Ridgeback puppy's process going, so find some basic steps to continue their education below:

- Introduce new sights, sounds, and smells. Your new Thai Ridgeback puppy is still learning all about this strange new world. It is your job to make sure that everything they experience is positive. No pressure! Expose your puppy to people, textures, noises, and places. It may sound silly, but they need to learn about carpet, hardwood, tile, and linoleum flooring. A puppy that has only been on carpeting may find slick flooring frightening. They should experience people that ride bikes and skateboards, wear sunglasses, wear a hat, or use an umbrella. The list for exposure is frankly endless, but try to find things that would represent the most likely things a puppy would have to learn about. For example, if you live in the city in a high-rise, your puppy may have to get used to things like fast movements, elevators, traffic noises, other dogs, all kinds of different people, different walking surfaces, construction equipment, buses, car horns, other loud noises, and places with crowds.

- Make sure all your Thai Ridgeback puppy's experiences are positive. Encourage them vocally with praise and hand out many treats. Tell them how brave they are. It is very important that you remain calm because dogs can read our emotions, and if you are feeling nervous, your puppy will pick up on that and wonder if they should be nervous too.

- Involve the entire family in the process. Your Thai Ridgeback puppy should know that they may encounter new things no matter which family member they happen to be with.

- Take things slowly. You don't want to do too much too quickly and overwhelm your Thai Ridgeback puppy. If you want to introduce new people, do it a person or two at a time and do not take them to a party with 50 people. If your puppy does become overwhelmed, they may become fearful.

- Gradually move outside of their comfort zone. Once your Thai Ridgeback puppy has been introduced to some new things and is feeling pretty confident, it may be time to start taking them on a trip to the pet store or to a friend's home for a scheduled puppy playdate. Of course, this cannot begin until your Thai Ridgeback puppy's vaccination series is over with. You should avoid heavily public places until your vaccination series is complete in order to reduce the risk of your puppy being exposed to infectious diseases.

- You could also opt to attend puppy classes, which focus not only on exposure to different things, but the lessons may help them understand basic commands more quickly.

- Those daily walks are important. Just being out and about will expose your Thai Ridgeback puppy to what is going on in the world around them.

- Always expose your Thai Ridgeback to a wide variety of people. You are really doing a disservice to your dog if they only hang out with one person. They will be wary of anyone that isn't you, and that can bring trouble should you want to go on vacation and hire a pet sitter or have a family member watch your dog. They can act out of fear and even show aggression.

- Use caution and common sense. You may have a good friend with a puppy, but is it a good idea to introduce a mini pinscher to a great dane? Keep sizes in mind when beginning those first introductions, and know any signs of discomfort your Thai Ridgeback may be showing you such as excessive panting, tucking their tail between their legs, having their ears backward and flat against their head, or excessive yawning. '

What Should You Do if Your Thai Ridgeback Puppy Seems Afraid?

When not everything goes according to plan, your Thai Ridgeback might seem fearful of something they experience in everyday life. You will have to come up with a plan should you have to try and ease your pet's fears. For example, if your puppy seems to be afraid of the vacuum cleaner, remove it and turn it on in another room while another family member comforts your pup and hands out some yummy treats.

Dogs retain a primitive fight or flight reflex despite thousands of years of domestication. The more fearful a dog becomes, the more their flight response will surface. If not socialized properly, a fearful dog may turn that fear into aggressive behavior and growl or bite when feeling cornered.

Feeling Overwhelmed

You could be feeling a bit overcome, especially if no one in your family has ever owned a dog before. If you have concerns over your ability to train or socialize your Thai Ridgeback, you can enroll them in a training school to help you provide everything your new puppy might need.

Your veterinarian may have some suggestions for reputable schools to help you succeed with your new best friend. You can always stay and observe a training class and see if it is a good fit for you. There is no shame in looking for help, but if you want to receive training alongside your pup, you might want to look into obedience classes. These classes will not only offer you training suggestions, but will offer safe socialization with other dogs too. Often puppies will need to retake the class, but it's normal and nothing to be concerned about.

Chapter Four: Feeding Your Thai Ridgeback

When you are planning to be a Thai Ridgeback puppy owner for the first time in your life, you might find yourself asking certain questions such as: what would your Thai Ridgeback puppy eat? How many times do you need to feed it? What would be a healthy treat? How many treats can you give them in a day? Well, it is a complex discussion and you need to be well equipped to face all these ordeals.

Today, the choices are endless and walking down the aisle in the dog section of your pet store is not going to prove much help. Gone are the days when there were only either/or.

Although it is a good thing; research over the years have developed supplements, dieting formulas, quality mineral and vitamin fortification. Although the primary function of all this varied diet is to provide a balanced diet and is essential in maintaining the health of your pup. The other use of such a variety is the success they bring to the entire training process.

The importance of food in the training process is highly underrated. The truth that very few people understand and the trainers too fail to mention is that the training process gets affected seriously if the puppy is overfed or underfed.

It is best to have a predictable feeding routine for the puppy so that they can be happy in the anticipation of food and also trusts you more on providing food to them leading to a loving relationship.

But, despite the obvious reason why you should choose quality ingredients for your Thai Ridgeback – which is providing your puppy with a balanced diet rich in essential nutrients, something else can benefit from balanced meals besides your puppy's health, and that is its training success.

Many dog owners overlook the importance that food has over the process of training, but the truth is, even the simplest directions can take a lot of time to teach if your pup is under or overfed. The eating and sleeping cycle can also give information about their excretion patterns.

Basics of Dog Nutrition

Many dog owners make the mistake of thinking that feeding their dogs "human foods" means they love them more. But, while they might have the best intentions, this can actually do a lot more harm than good. There are several things you need to know about dog nutrition, but here are the basics:

- Human food is too rich and contains many ingredients that can be harmful to dogs.
- Rich human food can cause potentially fatal conditions like pancreatitis.
- Obesity is just as dangerous for dogs as it is for humans. Without a balanced diet formulated for dogs, it is easy for your dog to gain too much weight.
- Dog foods formulated for puppies are not just smaller than adult food. They are specially formulated with more calories and protein, etc., to support all the growing your dog is doing!
- Most dog food bags have feeding guidelines on them that are based on weight. Make sure you weigh your

dog from time to time to ensure you are feeding them the right amount.

- Some dogs have food sensitivities and allergies, but these can be hard to diagnose without an elimination diet. If your dog is having tummy trouble, speak to your vet. They can probably recommend a food with a protein like salmon or lamb that is easier to digest.
- Only ever feed your dog-approved and safe dog treats!

Along with properly formulated food, your Thai Ridgeback needs fresh, clean water. Dogs do not need milk, and cows' milk can easily trigger tummy trouble – even in puppies!

Human Foods That Are Dangerous for Thai Ridgebacks

Sometimes, your Thai Ridgeback will have gastrointestinal symptoms even if you have not fed them something they should not have had. Dogs and puppies can be very sneaky, though, and they do love human food! So, an accidental nibble of certain human foods isn't out of the realm of possibilities. I have already discussed this in the "dog-proofing section", but it's worth mentioning again.

Inadvertent eating of that foods can at times be a cause for a medical emergency, so if you suspect your Thai Ridgeback has had any of these, go to the vet right away:

- Chocolate, especially dark chocolate

- Onions and garlic

- Sugar-free gum or any product with the artificial sweetener Xylitol

- Grapes and raisins

- Fruit pips and seeds, including cherry pits and apple seeds.

- Alcohol

- Coffee and tea (and any other caffeinated beverages)

- Avocados

- Macadamia nuts

- Salt

- Tomato and rhubarb leaves and stems

- Bread dough (not toxic, but can "rise" inside the gut, causing a blockage)

Tiny amounts of these foods, in some cases, won't do severe or permanent damage. But even just a few pieces of gum, for instance, can be fatal.

If your Thai Ridgeback has eaten something they should not have, always seek medical attention as soon as possible. This is NOT the time for a wait-and-see approach!

The Feeding Schedule

Now comes the essential question of how much the Thai Ridgeback should eat. This is extremely important as research indicates and so does common sense that out of love many owners over feed their small pups. The pups then have found to refuse more during the training session, because it does not want any reward. But to avoid all this hassle and mistakes, one simply needs to stick to a consistent routine for the first year of the puppy.

- 6 to 10 Weeks – 4 feedings a day
- 10 Weeks to 4 Months – 3 feedings a day
- 4 to 6 Months – 2 feedings a day
- 6 to 12 Months – Once it is 6 months feedings drop to only once a day.

What to Feed and How Much?

Dog food and puppy food is not the same thing, just like baby food and adult food is different in humans. Puppy food has been made with special care that takes care of the needs of a growing pup. If one switches to adult food early in the life of the pup, it can compromise on a lot of nutrients.

If you are thinking that if spending the big bucks for better quality really creates a difference; this is not as simple. Although better quality sure means that the pup will be subjected to a higher nutritional diversity but you could also concern the veterinarian in order to figure out how to mix and match in order to create the healthiest meals for your pup.

Now again the question of how much to provide. The schedule provided earlier is a measure of the number of feedings but for example if your dog is small, then the amount of the serving in one feeding is to be smaller than for the big dogs. You should also keep a watch on the pup and through trial and error find out the right amount of serving that your puppy needs. If the puppy skips a meal or does not eat food, mostly you would need to reduce one serving.

The Treats

The treats are the most important factor in the process of positive training. Without these tasty rewards, your pup will not be encouraged to participate in the sessions and go through all the trouble of getting your directions right.

But, what exactly is a treat? Should you pay tons of money for the most expensive smelly bones just for the sake of luring your pooch to show a shred of interest in the training? Of course, not. The treat can be pretty much anything your Thai Ridgeback loves to eat, even regular dog food. In fact, most dog trainers suggest that the treat should be a mixture of regular food and more special pieces of treats.

The most important thing is for the treats to be:

- Chewy
- Rich in Aroma and Flavor
- Easy to Break
- Soft

Start with a small number of treats and mix them up with doggy food. As the training progresses, increase the treats gradually. Also, make sure to use different treats on a weekly basis, so that your pup doesn't lose interest for cooperating. Treats can be pretty much anything your Thai

Ridgeback puppy enjoys – from special bone-shaped doggy treats, to small pieces of cheese or sausage.

Complete Balanced Diet

If you decide to cook for your Thai Ridgeback, or supplement his dry food diet with whole foods, remember that a complete and balanced diet does not need to be achieved at every, single meal. As it is with people, meeting balanced nutritional needs is something that is accomplished over time as an accumulation of good food choices made every day. So, the accumulative result of eating a wholesome variety of healthy foods over, as in a week's time, results in a balanced diet.

High quality dry puppy food is already formulated to meet the nutritional needs of puppies. Supplementing commercial puppy food with whole foods will complement your pup's diet with natural nutritional sources. In this way, your Thai Ridgeback can have the benefit of both.

Puppies Need Water

A Thai Ridgeback puppy needs access to fresh, clean water at all times. The rapid growth rate and active metabolism of a puppy makes his need for water a vital concern. A pup needs more water per pound of body weight than an adult dog.

A pup on a dry food diet will also have an increased need for water consumption for adequate digestion.

Refresh you Thai Ridgeback's water bowl several times a day with clean water, and make sure to wash the bowl each time to reduce the risk of disease. Also, depending on the source of your water, filtered water may taste better to a puppy than regular tap water.

The best dog water bowls are made of stainless steel. They are durable and easy to thoroughly keep clean.

Monitor consumption throughout the day to make sure your puppy is drinking plenty of water.

Preventing Food Aggression

Dogs can be very defensive like any other pet, particularly at supper time. Aggression to food makes pets display acts of being defensive over their food. It can turn into an issue for those living with the pet as they could be in danger of being nibbled, and it could prompt your puppy to become possessive in different parts of their life.

Food aggression is an environmental response a puppy encounters when eating suppers or treats, in which they utilize threatening behavior to monitor their food. This problem is very normal in puppies. Almost 20% of all puppies give indications of food aggression. This usually occurs if the dog is scared of not having a meal. There are ways of treating food aggression in puppies by appropriately preparing your puppy and dealing with their conduct. You can likewise find ways to anticipate it completely.

A few recognizing indications of food aggression are classified into three levels of destructiveness: Mild, moderate, and extreme.

Verbal signs best perceive the gentle level of food aggression. Your puppy might snarl when you approach them or their food while they are eating. They might likewise kick up some dust or raise their temper. A moderate level of food aggression is portrayed by a puppy snapping or rushing when an individual or other animal comes close to them while eating food. Extreme food aggression can be risky to individuals or different pets, as the puppy will start biting the apparent danger away.

If your Thai Ridgeback is showing any of these signs, you can feel guaranteed that this cautious conduct can be removed through a little effort. First of all, think about fixing the health of your pet. Chemicals can be the reason for such aggression, and fixing the levels might decrease this problem. Another choice for treatment is through training. Many pets with food aggression can be put through training divided into seven phases. Following are these seven stages to assist you in ending food aggression in your Thai Ridgeback:

Get your puppy used to your essence when eating

This step helps familiarize your pet with your essence when they are eating suppers or treats. Stack back from your pet by a couple of feet while they eat food from a bowl on the floor. The objective is to have your pet eating casually for at least ten dinners in succession before moving on to the next step.

Stand close, and have a chat with your pet.

This step centers on being close to your pet and having a discussion. While your pet is eating from their bowl, remain close to them and give them an exceptional treat. Address them in a conversational tone and ask them what they are eating or getting some information about their food are both great choices. Walk away from your puppy after giving them the treat. Keep practicing this cycle like clockwork. If your pet can stay calm and relaxed while eating for at least ten suppers in succession, you can continue to the following phase of this training.

Try feeding your pet through your hand.

Feeding with your hands is an important part of this step. It is significant for your Thai Ridgeback to comprehend that you are not representing a danger to their food when they eat. Approach your little guy, addressing them in a friendlier tone than the last stage. Remain close to their bowl, holding a hand out with a treat for your doggy. Rather than setting the treat in their bowl, urge your pet to eat the treat from your hand. After they take the treat, you can go back to your seat. Every day, attempt and twist down further until your hand is right close to their bowl as your pet takes the treat from you. You can move on to the next stage after getting ten successful results in succession.

Touch the bowl of your dog, yet do not take food away from it.

Address them in a relaxed tone, and place the treat with one hand. With the other, contact their bowl. However, do not take food from it. This will assist your Thai Ridgeback with becoming familiar with your nearby presence during eating times. Continue to the next part of the training if your puppy is feeling relaxed while eating for at least ten dinners straight.

Lift their bowl off the ground to give them their treat.

This stage is huge with regards to developing trust. You will lift their bowl from the beginning and give them a treat during this step. Address your pet in a quiet tone as you get their bowl. Every day, you will aim to lift the bowl higher until you can put it up on a table to set up the treat. Practice this step until you can walk relatively close and can put your puppy's bowl back in a similar spot from which you got it. This will build up trust among you and your Thai Ridgeback, and they should turn out to be completely open to eating around you before the end of this part.

Repeat the above procedure with every member of the house.

You need to make each and every family member repeat the procedure. This will develop trust with every person in the family. This will help you completely remove the food aggression problems from your Thai Ridgeback.

While your little dog might be open to eating around you, they may not be around other relatives or visitors that visit your home. Try establishing a protected climate for your puppy to eat for this situation. This incorporates separate dishes for each pet, isolating them at eating times or giving a gated area to your puppy to partake in their food.

Chapter Five: Grooming Your Thai Ridgeback

Bathing Your Puppy

Did you know that a lot of dog owners actually over-bathe their dogs? This is the most common mistake as humans don't want a dirty dog lying in their bed or furniture. Shockingly enough, dogs don't need to be bathed often. Veterinarians actually recommend pet owners to bathe their dogs only once every three months. Dogs that are more active, have longer hair, or is constantly rolling in dirt can be bathed more frequently but an average dog will benefit from being bathed once every few months. Keep in mind that frequent bathing and washing can irritate your pup's skin and causing medical conditions like dandruff.

Learning how and where to wash your dog properly is important as well. Those who own smaller breeds of dogs have the advantage of just washing them in the sink or bathtub. However, if your dog is of a larger breed, like Thai Ridgebacks, obviously they can't fit in the sink. Portable doggy tubs are a good option if the weather is warm outside. If not, most pet stores actually offer a free dog washing station. Usually, this will consist of a large area with removable nozzles used to spray down your dog. Some people have the option of washing their dog in their yard with the garden hose. However, the water that comes out of your garden hose is likely cold and unless it's really hot outside, your dog probably doesn't enjoy being bathed in ice-cold water.

So, how exactly do you wash your Thai Ridgeback properly? This is important to learn so you don't go into the situation unprepared. Having a well-trained dog is important for this task as it is easiest when they are calm and sitting still. If your dog is not trained well, you may want to put them through behavioral training before taking on a task like this. Here are a few tips on how to bathe your pup properly:

- Brush your dog's hair/fur before the bath. Make sure your dog doesn't have any matted hair as it tends to hold lots of water. Washing your dog with matted hair will cause skin irritation. If you aren't able to brush or cut out those mats by yourself, it is recommended to take them to a professional groomer to have it done. Do not attempt to brush or cut out any mats if you aren't confident. Before you start the bath, you can put a large cotton ball in your dog's ear to help keep out water. This will prevent ear infections or irritations.

- Use lukewarm water to bathe your dog. Although humans typically shower with hot water, your dog's skin is different from ours. The water you use should not be hotter than what you would use to wash a baby. Make sure that the water is not hot to touch but is a comfortable warmth.

- Talk to your Thai Ridgeback calmly during the bath. For dogs that are feisty during bath time, try to soothe them by talking to them gently. Don't yell, shout, or panic during this time as they may misunderstand the situation as being intimidating. After a few baths they will learn that you are not trying to harm them and it can be quite an enjoyable experience.

- Use dog shampoo when bathing your Thai Ridgeback. Dog shampoo dries out skin less than what human shampoo would. Lather the shampoo gently into your dog's body and massage it all over. Be careful not to get any shampoo in their eyes as it is extremely irritating.

- Rinse well. Make sure you are rinsing your dog until there are no more soap suds on its body. Any shampoo left on your dog's body after the bath can irritate its skin.

- Air dry your Thai Ridgeback after the bath. Avoid using blow dryers to dry your dog's fur. Blow dryers tend to be too hot for a dog's skin. If needed, there are blow-dryers that are designed for dogs that you can purchase. These blow dryers expel air in lower temperatures that won't cause irritation.

- Reward your Thai Ridgeback after the bath. Follow up the bath with lots of praise, petting, play, or treats. This will help your dog associate bath time to a reward which will make them less irritable during the process. A lot of the times your dog may be frustrated after the bath so encouraging exercise afterward can help your dog blow off some steam.

If you have a dog that is particularly bad with baths, you can explore the option of taking him/her to a professional groomer. If your dog requires a strenuous wrestle and a difficult struggle to keep him/her in the bath, it may be a better option to have a professional do it. Groomers will not only just give them a bath but they will clip your puppy's nails, clean their buttocks area, trim hair near the eyes, and clean their ears as well. A lot of groomers are priced reasonably and do such a great job that you won't have to go back for another few months.

If you have a dog that is a long hair breed like Poodles, Maltese, or Yorkies it is a 100% must to have them groomed by a professional. Since these breeds have hair and not fur, they don't shed their hair and it keeps growing just like a human. Eventually, they will have to get it cut to make sure it doesn't dread. If you have Thai Ridgeback pup, groomers are still helpful if your dog strongly dislikes baths. Groomers have the equipment and other professionals to help make the experience as smooth and as quick as possible. Overall, bathing is important to help keep your pup's skin and coat healthy, clean, and free of parasites. Depending on the breed and the environment you're in, some dogs may require more frequent baths. When in doubt, advise your local veterinarian to get a proper schedule on when and how often you should be bathing your Thai Ridgeback.

Brushing Your Dog's Teeth

Did you know that the most common disease for dogs is not heartworms or rabies, but it is actually gum disease? Gum disease is formed in the dog's gums and is caused by the buildup of tartar on their teeth. If not properly treated, your dog is at risk of bacterial infections that could be lethal. The easiest way to avoid this is to brush your Thai Ridgeback dog's teeth often. Every day if you have the time. This is an important part of puppy hygiene that people tend to overlook as it is time-consuming and difficult. In most cases, people will use a doggy toothbrush to do this but if you are on a time crunch, veterinarians recommend just using your fingers to get the tartar out of your pup's teeth. I know it sounds gross but this is important to prevent bacterial infection. It is important to start training your dog when they are young to be comfortable with teeth brushing. This way there are less likely to develop gum disease and prevent bad behaviors like chewing on objects or other people.

Below I will provide you with a set of directions to make the teeth brushing process a little easier and more comfortable for you and your canine friend.

- Get a doggy toothbrush. There should be a wide variety of them at any pet store. Doggy toothbrushes have softer bristles that are made to give you easier access to the teeth that are harder to reach. Make sure to choose a toothbrush based on your dog's size. Obviously bigger dogs will require a larger toothbrush and smaller dogs will need a smaller one that can fit into their mouth. Like we mentioned earlier, using your finger to clean your Thai Ridgeback dog's teeth is also a good option. There are products called finger brushes that fit onto the end of your finger which can give you better accuracy and precision during the brush. However, you may risk getting bit by your dog by using this technique. Avoid using human toothbrushes for your dog as the bristles are too hard and may damage your dog's mouth, tongue, or gums. If you aren't able to find a doggy toothbrush, you can use a child's toothbrush with extra soft bristles.

- Use doggy toothpaste. Just like toothbrushes, there is a variety of different doggy toothpaste at your local pet stores that are made specifically for dogs. Never use human toothpaste to brush your Thai Ridgeback dog's teeth. Human toothpaste usually contains fluoride and other chemicals that are toxic to dogs. It is not harmful to us as we don't usually swallow our toothpaste but many dogs will swallow toothpaste as their teeth are being brushed. Doggy toothpaste is also made in different flavors that your dog may enjoy to help make the process of brushing easier. Feel free to try different flavors to find one that best suits you and your puppy.

- Get your Thai Ridgeback comfortable with you having your hand in or near its mouth. When you first start brushing your dog's teeth, take it slow and get your dog used to you being around its mouth area. When training your dog, get him/her used to you touching their muzzle area. It may take some time for your dog to get used to it but once they are, it is a lot less nerve-wracking for your dog.

- Start the toothbrushing process by letting your Thai Ridgeback lick and taste a small amount of the doggy toothpaste from your finger. This will help you understand how well your puppy likes the toothpaste. It will also help your dog get used to the taste of the toothpaste which will make him/her more likely to be comfortable in the process.

- Next, show the doggy toothbrush to your dog and let him/her sniff it and inspect it. Allow your Thai Ridgeback to lick some of the toothpaste off the toothbrush. Make sure to praise your dog after this as it will positively reinforce this action.

- In this step, begin to gently brush your pup's teeth. Start with the ones that are the easiest to reach. Their canine teeth are the longest and the easiest to reach. Gently lift up your puppy's upper lip and brush their teeth gently back and forth. Do this gently and slowly to help your dog get used to the feeling of having a toothbrush on their teeth and gums. If your dog is reluctant or aggressive during the brushing, proceed with caution. To make it easier, have a friend or a family member help calm your pup as you brush their teeth. Remember to reward your dog after a few minutes of brushing and reward them again at the end.

- Brush the outside of your Thai Ridgeback dog's teeth. Once your dog has gotten used to the gentle brushing it is time to combine a few actions. Place some more toothpaste on your toothbrush and gradually brush along the entire outside surface of the upper and lower teeth. You can increase the number of teeth every time you brush. Make sure to brush along the gum line as well.

- Once you have brushed all of your Thai Ridgeback dog's teeth make sure to brush the inside surfaces of your dog's teeth. Place one hand over the top of your dog's muzzle, lift their upper lips and open his/her mouth. Once their mouth is open, start brushing the bottom of their upper teeth and the top of their lower teeth.

- Make teeth brushing into a daily routine. The more often you brush your dog's teeth the more he/she will get used to it. This will make teeth brushing easier over time.

Nail Trimming

Trimming dog nails is another important part of grooming. The thing is, if you leave their nails to grow too long, they can have problems walking, arthritis and end up curving into a pad of their foot. That is quite uncomfortable and painful when they walk.

Generally, you must plan to trim their nails at least once a month. Others with fast nail growth might need frequent nail trimming than the others.

For instance, medium or large pups like Thai Ridgebacks that often walk on the sidewalks or asphalt for more than an hour every day often have their nails wear down and hence, need little trimming aside from their dew claws. Small pups tend to go for shorter walks, and their nails need to be trimmed every couple of weeks.

Realize that they have veins in their nails. This means that, when trimming the nails, you should not cut them too short as that might quickly hurt and cause them to bleed. If they don't get their nails trimmed often enough, they risk having their veins grow too long, hence the need to take them off a little bit at a time. After that, we encourage trimming their veins little by little every week to promote the vein to shrink back into the nails.

To do this, you can use clippers or grinders. If you use clippers, simply position them in a way that you can easily flip their paw back and look under it. Then trim a little bit at a time. If they have white nails, you can quickly see the inside of the nail to determine where to cut. However, if the nails are black, cutting will take a little more time.

If the dog nails are short and smooth, it is best if you use nail grinders to avoid cutting them too fast. The nail grinders can be very loud and could scare your dog. Therefore, it is better if you introduce them gradually until they are used to it. You could also buy the styptic powder to stop bleeding in case you cut into the vein. Alternatively, you can use corn starch or flour to stop bleeding.

Ear Cleaning

You should clean your Thai Ridgeback dog's ears at least every 2-4 weeks to prevent infections. This is very important, especially because they have long ears and these kinds of breeds are prone to infections. In other words, the frequency with which you clean their ears will depend on the breed and the amount of ear wax they secrete.

For most pups, cleaning the ears once a month is often enough. However, if they have long ears and likes to swim, you may have to do it every fortnight.

Tips for cleaning ears

Start by preparing your Thai Ridgeback dog's ears for grooming by simply brushing them to remove matted or dirty hair

If there is excessive hair around the canal, it is advisable to seek the help of a professional to help remove it. This is because if you remove the hair around the ear incorrectly, you risk damaging their ears

The most important thing as far as cleaning ears goes is to do gently and with caution. Remember that the ear is a very delicate organ. Only use a formulated solution to clean the ear.

Begin by dripping small amounts of pooch-friendly ear solution and massage the bottom of the ear before you move on to the other one. Then allow the dog to shake to get rid of the solution once you clear the solution, dab cotton wool to get rid of the excess on the outside of the ear canal and any wax.

Caution: DO NOT use anything inside the ear canal.

Chapter Six: Training and Behavior Modification

Short, regular training sessions combined with a strong bond with your Thai Ridgeback will make training an enjoyable experience for both of you.

Why Bonding Is Important

Many dog owners assume that their dog's love and trust are automatic. While it is true that dogs are naturally affectionate, a strong bond between dog and owner takes work. Nurturing your bond with your dog has many benefits for you and the dog. Your dog will be easier to train, listen more attentively, and be calmer overall when he feels secure in his relationship with you. Bonding with your dog is not just good for your dog—your quality of life will improve as well. Research supports the common idea that dog ownership, especially when a strong bond exists between the dog and owner, has positive physical and emotional effects.

The good news is that the important work of bonding with your dog can be easy and enjoyable! Use one (or all) of the following suggestions to strengthen your bond with your Thai Ridgeback:

1. *Talk to your dog.* Talking to your Thai Ridgeback is a great way to bond. Many dogs understand quite a few words, and dogs have been shown to read body language and tone better than we do. Your dog will be able to pick up on your mood and may even help improve it. Dogs make a great, nonjudgmental sounding board.

2. *Be consistent.* Your dog will be calmer and better behaved if he is sure of the rules. Consistency in your expectations and routine will help him feel secure in his place. Scheduling walk- and mealtimes will be good for you both.

3. *Play together every day.* Puppies especially love to play. Make time each day to play fetch, toss around a

Frisbee, or teach him a new trick. Nothing will build a bond faster than good, old-fashioned play.

4. *Look him in the eye.* Research has shown that looking your dog in the eye strengthens the bond between owner and pet. Meeting gazes causes an increase in oxytocin levels (a hormone that promotes nurturing and attachment) in both the dog and his owner.

Keep It Short

Many short training sessions will be more successful long-term than the same practice crammed into one marathon session. Young dogs especially benefit from shorter training sessions with frequent breaks. This is not to say that training should be done five minutes at a time each day. A study by Demant et al. (2011) indicated that the ideal training schedule for retention is twice a week, with each training session broken up into smaller chunks of time. Aim for 4-5 sessions of 10 minutes (or shorter if your dog loses interest) twice a week. This will allow you to plan training around your work and travel schedule while allowing your dog time to rehearse the training during sleep.

The primary goal in training should be to reinforce positive behaviors, both with rewards and consistency.

Mistakes and defiance are more likely when your dog is physically and mentally exhausted. Be consistent in your training while giving your dog time to rest. The dogs in the Demant et al. study (2011) all learned the commands over a four-week period, but those that were trained twice a week in a higher number of shorter sessions acquired the skills faster and with less resistance.

Positive Reinforcement

All of the methods described in this guide are part of positive-reinforcement-based dog training. I have found that being harsh with your dog and focusing on punishing bad behavior does not do anything to help the situation and often makes dogs afraid of training altogether. While repeated bad behaviors can be frustrating, you should refrain from yelling at your Thai Ridgeback dog, locking them in unfamiliar cages, or otherwise making negative associations with training exercises. This only shows that working with you is not fun, exciting, or good for them, and they will not want to cooperate better in the future.

We will cover positive ways to correct behavior later, but you should try to focus on reinforcing good actions and ignoring bad ones in general. This means rewarding your dog when they get something right, like peeing outside or behaving well on a leash. When they get it wrong, like peeing inside or going crazy on their walk, they do not get the treat they expect and will remember this. This is much more productive when it comes to learning right vs. wrong behaviors, and your dog will come away from the training with a better impression of you as their leader.

Remember to bring patience and understanding with you to every training session. Your puppy, no matter what age or stage of training they are in, will mess up and run into problems along the way. Even the most well-behaved and expertly trained dogs get confused sometimes or don't remember what to do. Take a step back when something isn't clicking, and try to approach it from a new angle. Consider how your training could change to adapt to your dog, or if there's something else in the dog's life that might be causing a relapse in bad behavior. There are always solutions to a pup's misbehavior that do not involve harsh treatment or repeated punishment.

Reading Your Dog's Body Language

Training will be more successful when you and your Thai Ridgeback are both relaxed and happy. An overly stressed or nervous dog will not learn or perform well, leading to bad habits and frustration. Look for the following signs of your dog's mood:

Relaxed: When your Thai Ridgeback is comfortable, he will stand with his head high and his legs loose. His tail will be down and relaxed. Any tail movement will be a gentle sway. His tongue may be lolling out of his mouth because his mouth will be open slightly. Some dog breeds even appear to be smiling when they are happy. This is the ideal state for training.

Playful: A Thai Ridgeback that is feeling playful will have a hard time holding still. His tail will be up and wagging, often so quickly that his entire backside wiggles. He may be moving toward you or he may lean forward while bending his front legs. He will often bark or jump toward you by way of invitation. In this state, your dog is ready to run and play. He will be too wound up to pay proper attention. Spend a few minutes playing before attempting to calm him down.

Curious/alert: Any new smells or situations will cause your Thai Ridgeback to enter this state. He will assess the situation and determine if the environment is friendly. Most dogs will point their ears up and forward when curious or alert. He may cock his head to one side. He will stand firmly, leaning forward slightly. His tail will be up but not stiff. A dog will not stay in this position for long. Once your dog has evaluated the potential threat, he will either relax or prepare to fight or flee.

Aggressive: When your Thai Ridgeback responds to potential threats with aggression, his tail will be stiff and his hair may seem to stand on end. He will curl his lips so his teeth are visible. He may or may not accompany this stance with a growl.

Submissive: A submissive or fearful Thai Ridgeback will often make his body small in order to appear non-threatening. His tail will be down and may curl under his body. He will lower his body and lay his ears back. He will not maintain direct eye contact and may only peer out of the corners of his eyes, exposing mostly the whites. He may lick at the dominant person or dog to show submission.

Learning to read your Thai Ridgeback dog's body language is one of the best ways to be sure he is ready to learn a new skill or practice training. Use your own body language and tone to help your dog be relaxed and attentive before attempting any training. This will go a long way to preventing a negative training session.

Housebreaking Your Puppy

Housebreaking your puppy can seem like a monumental job. It does take quite a bit to teach your puppy that it is okay to toilet in the house, but it must be a specific location.

Puppy Pads are great for housebreaking your puppy. If you intend on letting your Thai Ridgeback toilet in the house, you want to make certain it is not on the carpet or hardwood floor. You also want to provide a place he/she can relieve themselves throughout the day that is not their bed.

Your puppy does not want to be in a crate with defecation and pee, while also having to sleep there. If you have a puppy breed, you can trust not to chew the entire house apart in boredom, then housebreak your puppy.

Lay out a clear place, using puppy pads. A puppy pad may have an odor. Many have a fragrance to avoid the ammonia smell in the home. If your puppy does not go on the pad even after training, consider that it might be the smell of the pad that makes it the wrong place for your puppy.

After all, what smells great to you, may truly irritate your dog's sense of smell.

Step by Step on How to Housetrain your Thai Ridgeback

1. Clear out a room you are not using.

2. Put plastic over the entire floor.

3. Cover it with newspaper.

4. Place two or three puppy pads in the room.

5. Place a puppy bed or crate for sleeping in the room.

6. Give your puppy food and water.

7. When your puppy indicates a need to relieve itself, carry him/her to the puppy pad.

8. If your dog tries to walk away or sniff another area, gently, and calmly, place your puppy back on the pad.

9. When your puppy goes on the pad, immediately provide a treat.

10. Repeat this process.

What to do when your Thai Ridgeback doesn't listen

You are bound to have some issues with housetraining your Thai Ridgeback. Simply showing your puppy the right pad and providing a treat, will not always do.

Your puppy may forget. He/she may wait too long. They may realize during the day they do not get treats and you are not there to stop them.

The good news is—you can get your puppy to go in the right place.

Leave a soiled pad in the room. It should be free of poo, but have a little ammonia smell to it. If you do not have a soiled pad, take a Q-tip outside with you the next time you take your puppy out. Swipe a bit of the urine from this bathroom break. Rub the Q-tip on the pad.

The scent will help your Thai Ridgeback investigate and find the right place to go to the bathroom.

Never yell at your puppy or make him/her feel embarrassed or ashamed.

Always pick up your puppy and bring him/her to the pad when you catch the puppy going in an improper place.

Also remember that the age of your puppy determines how frequently they need to go, as well as their size. If you know when your puppy went last, then you can time when they will need to go again.

This way, you are on hand to help your puppy find the right location.

Clean up the wrongly soiled location. Use a pet cleaner, so the odor is completely removed.

Always praise or give treats when your puppy goes in the right location.

Eventually, you can use voice or clicker commands to help your Thai Ridgeback find the right place to toilet.

Make sure you provide a clean pad for your puppy in the same place, every time.

Bathroom Accidents due to Excitement

Housetraining has another side to it. There are times when your Thai Ridgeback is so young that excitement can cause him/her to go to the bathroom without meaning to do so.

If this happens, quickly bring your excited puppy to the area in the house they should go.

Your puppy can finish his/her business needs. You can also open the door and let your puppy go outside if an accident occurs. Quietly and calmly clean up the mess. Do not yell. Do not say "bad dog." Just clean it up. The next time your puppy goes reward him/her.

If your puppy is excited and holds his/her bladder, give him a treat.

Crate Training

We all want a well-behaved dog who doesn't destroy things and relieves himself outside, and crate training is a crucial part of that. A crate provides a safe environment for your dog, as well as a personal space.

While many people associate crates with being "confined," dogs are naturally denning animals who prefer to stay in enclosed, compact spaces. Crates give them a sense of safety, and when they're taught to use them from a young age, they can help soothe anxiousness.

You typically go to your couch or bedroom to decompress when you're upset, and a dog's crate provides a similar purpose for puppies. When dogs need to relax or snooze, they can use the crate as a safe place to go.

Because it will quickly become a valued haven for your dog, picking the right crate for his specific needs is critical. Let's look at what to look for while selecting the ideal crate for your dog. But first, why is crate training important?

Why Is Crate Training Important?

Crates, when used correctly, can be a valuable tool for the typical pet owner. Both you and your Thai Ridgeback can benefit from proper, constructive crate training.

Here are my top seven reasons for crate training your dog:

1. Provide a Secure Environment

Crates can provide a safe sanctuary for your dog when he is agitated or exhausted and requires some quiet. When your dog is in his crate, whether by his choice or by yours, children must be educated that he is out of bounds for them and must be left alone.

2. Assistance with House Training

Crates are excellent for housebreaking. Because dogs and puppies dislike a soiled bed, a correctly sized crate can help you teach him bladder and feces control.

3. Domestic Safety

It's good to have your dog napping nicely in his crate even though you're not there to oversee him. Perhaps you're preparing supper or renovating, and your dog is causing a hazard just by being underfoot. You'll have rest of mind knowing he's safely tucked away.

4. More Secure Travel

It is considerably safer for both of you to have your dog travel in a crate than to have him loose in the car.

5. More Convenient Vet Visits

If your dog has already been crate trained, he will be significantly less stressed if he is confined in the cage or run overnight at the veterinarian.

6. Limitation of Damage

Have you seen those internet "dog shaming" videos where the pet parent returns home to find his furnishings in shambles? Those mishaps may have been averted if the dog had been left in his crate with a bone or toy to gnaw on rather than trashing the designer couch.

7. Emergency Evacuation

Finally, having a crate-trained dog makes it much easier for everyone involved if you ever have to leave your home in a crisis or emergency. Whether you keep your puppy with you or have to leave him with others, he will be happier in his crate. He'll be more relaxed if he has his own blankets and toys with your scent on them, rather than an unfamiliar crate that is stressful for him.

What Are The Things To Look For In A Dog Crate

It's difficult for a new pet parent to know what to look for when selecting an ideal crate. To assist you, we've broken down the various materials, the size of a dog crate that should be used, and the optimal size for your dog.

When to use each of the four crate types

You'll come across four typical crate kinds when shopping for your pet's crate: wire, plastic, soft-sided, and wooden dog crates.

1. Wire crates are easily transportable and storable. For pets with long coats or those who live in hotter areas, this sort of enclosure allows plenty of airflow.

2. Plastic crates are made of a strong and long-lasting substance. This is great for families who frequently travel with some who must meet airline restrictions.

3. Soft-sided crates are ideal for small breed dogs or pups who are used to being confined. This confinement is simple to set up and takedown thanks to the lightweight and flexible materials.

4. Style-conscious families will appreciate wooden crates. They come in a number of styles that you may be able to integrate in your home decor for a long-term containment solution.

What size crate will be comfortable for my dog?

You may now have a better notion of what sort of crate is best for your dog, but you may still be unsure of what size crate to buy. Crates are available in numerous sizes to accommodate dogs of various shapes and sizes. Choose a dog crate that allows your dog to stand up, turn around, stretch out, and lie down when determining how big it should be. Any extra space will encourage your pet to sleep on one side of the box while disregarding the other.

Many crates come with recommended weight ranges, but you should consider your dog's physical attributes and weight. Although a long-legged Whippet and a chubby, short-legged Pembroke Welsh Corgi may weigh the same, the two breeds will have distinct requirements when it comes to selecting a suitable crate in which to sleep. Consider the height and length of the crates while you shop to choose one that is the most comfortable for your Thai Ridgeback pet.

We recommend following the steps below to establish the optimal measurements for the crate you purchase in order to best determine the size crate your Thai Ridgeback will require. After you've measured your dog, check the product specifications to discover which size is ideal for you.

- Measure your dog's length from the tip of his snout to the base of his tail while he is standing.
- Measure your dog's height from the top of his head to the ground while sitting.
- Add 4 inches to your dog's length and height measurements and use those values to shop for the proper crate dimensions.

When getting a puppy, bear in mind that he will grow! Expect to buy a larger crate as they develop, or estimate the proper crate size based on their projected adult size and search for a divider that can expand with your pup.

Consider the future while choosing a crate for your Thai Ridgeback. Choose a crate that your pet can grow into rather than one that fits their current size. If you choose this route, make sure the crate you buy has moveable crate dividers so you can adjust the amount of space for your puppy as he grows. You can also reduce the size of the crate by placing a cardboard box on one side of it until your pet outgrows it (however, if your puppy is a chewer, this may not be a good option for him).

The Crate Training Process

Crate training can take days or weeks, depending on your Thai Ridgeback dog's age. When crate training, keep two things in mind: the crate should always be associated with something nice, and training should be done in small steps. Don't go too fast.

Step 1: Teach your puppy how to use the crate.

Put the container in a family room or other section of the house where the family spends a lot of time. Place a comfortable blanket or a bed in the crate. Remove the door or prop it open to let the dog explore the crate at their leisure. Some dogs are naturally intrigued and will immediately begin napping in the crate.

- Bring them over to the box and talk to them in a pleasant tone of voice. Ensure the crate door is open and securely fastened to avoid hitting or frightening your dog.
- Place small treats near the crate door, then just inside the door, and then all the way inside to entice your dog to enter. If your puppy refuses to go all the way in at first, it's okay; don't push him.
- Continue to throw goodies into the crate until your dog walks quietly inside the crate to retrieve the food. If treats aren't appealing, try putting a beloved toy in the crate. This phase could take anywhere from a few minutes to several days.

Step 2: Feed your Thai Ridgeback in the crate.

After your dog has been introduced to his crate, start serving them their regular meals near it. This will create a pleasant connection with the crate.

- If your dog enters the crate easily when you start Step 2, place the full food dish or interactive puzzle toy at the far back of the crate.
- If he still refuses to enter, only place the dish inside as far as he can go without being frightened or concerned. Each time you feed him, move the dish further back in the crate.
- When your dog is standing comfortably in the crate, close the door while he eats. When you first do this, open the door as soon as he stops eating. Leave the door closed a few minutes longer with each successful feeding until he stays inside the crate for ten minutes or more after eating.
- If they begin whining to be let out, you may have increased the time too quickly. Try to let them stay in the crate for a shorter period of time next time.

Step 3: Try longer crating times.

While you're at home, you can confine your dog in the crate for short periods of time if he has been eating his regular meals there with no signs of anxiety or distress.

- Invite him to the crate and reward him with a treat.

- Use a speech cue to invite him in, such as "crate." With a treat in your hand, point to the interior of the crate to encourage him.
- Praise your dog as he enters the crate, then give him the treat and shut the door.
- Go into a separate room for a few minutes after sitting calmly near the crate for five to ten minutes. Return, sit gently for a few moments, and then release him.
- Repeat this process several times a day, progressively increasing the amount of time the dog spends in the box, as well as the amount of time you're out of sight.
- You can start keeping your dog in the crate when you leave for short periods of time and/or let him sleep there at night once he can stay quietly in the crate for more than 20 minutes with you mostly out of sight. This could take a few days or weeks.

Step 4, Part I: Crate your dog when you go out.

You can start putting your dog in the crate for short amounts of time when you leave the house after they can stay about 30 minutes without becoming anxious or fearful.

- Use your standard command and a treat to place them in the crate. You might also keep a few safe toys in the crate for them to play with.

- Change the time you put your dog in the crate during your "getting ready to leave" routine. Although they shouldn't be crated for an extended period of time before leaving, you can do so anywhere between five and 20 minutes before leaving.
- Don't make your departures emotional or lengthy; they should be brief. Praise your dog briefly before rewarding them with a treat for entering the crate.

When you get home, don't reward your dog for being excited by responding enthusiastically to them. Keep arrivals low-key to prevent increasing their anxiety about when you'll return. When you are at home, crate your dog for short periods so they don't link crating with being left alone.

Step 4, Part II: Crate your dog at night.

Use your regular command and a treat to encourage your dog to enter the crate. If you have a puppy, you might want to keep the crate in your bedroom or a neighboring corridor at first. Puppies regularly need to go out to relieve themselves late at night, and you'll want to be able to hear your dog alert you to let him out. To prevent associating the box with social isolation, older dogs should be kept out at first.

Once your dog is sleeping soundly in the crate near you at night, you can gradually move it to the desired location, though any time spent with your dog—even sleep time—is a chance to fortify your bond.

Is Your Thai Ridgeback Puppy Whining In His Crate

While there is no perfect way to totally eliminate whining behavior in pups, there are strategies to reduce it. It's crucial to perform good crate training and avoid instilling undesirable habits in your Thai Ridgeback early on.

Below are a few things you can do to help your Thai Ridgeback stop whining in his crate.

Don't pay attention to the whining.

One of the most common mistakes novice pet parents make is paying attention to their puppies or taking them out of the crate once they start whining. The best choice is to ignore whining. Any attention will just serve to reinforce the behavior.

Pet parents should wait until a puppy is quiet before giving him attention or letting him out of the crate. The idea is to teach the puppy that calm, quiet behavior leads to a reward. After waking up from his nap or a few minutes of peaceful behavior, the puppy can be released.

Choose the appropriate crate size.

Puppies should have enough room in their crates to feel safe and secure. The dog must have the ability to stand up, turn around, and play with toys in the crate.

Consider dog crates with dividers so you can change the size of the crate as your puppy gets bigger.

Make your Thai Ridgeback feel at ease in the crate.

One technique to lessen whimpering and anxiety in your puppy is to familiarize him with his crate.

The first rule is to introduce your dog to the crate gradually. Your Thai Ridgeback needs time to learn that the crate is a safe and happy place. If you start crating without giving him sufficient time to get to know you, he'll be more likely to object.

Never use the crate to punish your Thai Ridgeback. Treats, chew toys, and blankets in the crate will make the experience easier.

When your Thai Ridgeback is peaceful and quiet in his crate, praise him with dog treats. Most dogs will enter the crate on their own once they've become accustomed to it, so we recommend leaving the crate door open while it's not in use.

It becomes their secure refuge where they can relax, chew on toys, and watch their families.

Make sure there are lots of potty breaks.

Puppies are unable to "hold it" for as long as adult dogs, thus it is the job of the pet parent to ensure that young puppies have plenty of opportunities to go outside—even in the middle of the night.

Kennel soiling is frequently induced by leaving the puppy alone for an extended period of time. To know the number of hours a puppy needs between potty breaks, add his age plus one.

A two-month-old Thai Ridgeback puppy can normally hold it for three hours, while a three-month-old dog can usually hold it for four hours.

It's better to be safe than sorry, so estimate how long your puppy can go between potty breaks based on his age.

When it comes to potty training, there is no such thing as too many trips outside.

Don't forget to think about the crate location.

The position of your puppy's crate may influence whether or not he whines. Crate placement has a significant impact on a dog's response to it. If the crate is positioned in a distant room, or even worse, the garage or basement, the puppy may feel isolated and cry.

The box should be kept where the family spends a lot of time. Some pet parents choose to utilize two crates, one in the family room or living room and the other in the puppy's bedroom.

Keeping the crate handy will allow you to hear when your puppy wants to go outside and make your puppy feel less nervous.

Because most young pups can't hold it for the entire night, pet parents must be able to hear when their puppies wake up and cry to go outside. Otherwise, the puppy may be compelled to soil the crate.

Allow your Thai Ridgeback to have plenty of opportunities to run about.

Don't underestimate the power of playtime to keep your puppy from whining in the crate.

In addition to the kennel, make sure your puppy is getting plenty of activity and attention. If this is the case, your dog will most likely be ready for a nap while crated.

To keep your Thai Ridgeback occupied and avoid boredom, add interactive or dog treat toys to his or her box. When you crate your dog, give him a safe, hard, rubber busy toy loaded with a little peanut butter or a few goodies. This tasty routine, if followed consistently, may help your puppy enjoy going into the crate.

Pet parents can try a KONG puppy dog toy, but we recommend testing toys first to ensure your dog won't rip them up.

When To Worry About A Puppy Crying In His Crate

While puppy whining is common, whether a dog is crated or not, pet parents should be aware of any excessive whining or unusual behavior.

If whining is new behavior for a dog who has previously handled being crated well, or if you detect any other concerning signs, contact your veterinarian.

We agree that pet caregivers should be vigilant and seek assistance if puppy crying persists. Some puppy whining in the kennel is normal. It's critical to contact a trainer or veterinary behaviorist if a puppy is reactive the entire time he's crated—no matter how long he's been there—or hurts himself in an attempt to escape.

Command Training Vs. Treat Training Your Dog

Many dog owners will use treats with the wrong technique. Treat training has its time and place but without the correct timing it can lead to more unwanted behavior. Every dog deserves a treat but you first must understand your dog. Is it food motivated? Does it only do what you ask for a treat? If the answer is "Yes, my dog is food motivated," then you have to slowly train it off of treats. It is true that treats can aid in teaching manners and behavior in dogs, however, if your Thai Ridgeback only pays attention to a command with a treat in sight, and not you, its pack leader, then this can only lead to future problems. The pack leader always controls the food. A dog owner must always keep this in mind when using treats. A dog will quickly learn how to manipulate its owner to receive a treat.

Treat Training Your Thai Ridgeback: The Downside

- **If you opt to treat train, you MUST have a treat with you 24/7:** If you make your Thai Ridgeback dance to the tune of treats, you will have to keep a few treats handy all the time to make your dog pay attention to you and your directions.
    - Your dog will simply not listen to you if you do not have a treat, which increases your dog's dependence on treats.
- **Dog focuses on treats only:** When you use treats to teach your Thai Ridgeback obedience and respect, your dog's attention mainly focuses on the treat. Since the treats are tempting, your dog will do everything possible to get it and may end up not paying attention to your actual command. I always ask for my dog's attention to be on me before he receives the treat. Only when and after his eyes are connected to mine, he may then receive the treat.
- **The dog becomes lazy:** Treat training your Thai Ridgeback also makes your dog lazy because your dog will pay attention to you only when you have a treat, and will not otherwise listen to you or obey you.
- **Wrong timing results in unwanted behaviors:** Treat training is very tricky because you need to be

particular about the timing of the treat; if you fail to deliver a treat to your puppy at the right time, it could result in unacceptable and undesirable behaviors.

- **Treats make your dog greedy:** Treats do not inculcate a positive and respectful behavior in your dog. Rather, they make your dog treat greedy.

- **It upsets your dog's digestive system and housebreaking schedule:** Using treats to train your dog is not advisable because a constant supply of treats upsets your dog's digestive system and gets in the way of your housebreaking schedule.

It is always possible to use treats as a training tool but it is wise to first fully understand the technique. You may feel the urge to give your puppy treats to gain acceptance and to increase your bond with it. In doing so, you not only lose the power of this reward system tool, but you will teach your Thai Ridgeback to expect treats from you instead of being ready to complete a task for a treat.

Fortunately, there is a much better, useful, and effective alternative to using treats to train your puppy.

The Alternative: Command Training

A fantastic substitute to using treats to obedience train your Thai Ridgeback is using verbal commands. Command training refers to using verbal commands to train you dog. Keep in mind that the energy you project towards your puppy will determine the success of the command. Your puppy will always move towards calm, strong leadership. Giving a command with this energy will ensure a better outcome. Try to keep this energy in mind when teaching your puppy new commands.

If you want your Thai Ridgeback to come to you, you will use the command 'come' or 'come here' to tell your dog you need it to approach you; this verbal command will replace using a treat to show your dog you need it to approach you.

Using verbal commands do not inculcate undesirable behavior in your dog because you can employ any material object to train your dog to do something.

Using this method, you teach your dog to behave in a certain manner by using your voice. Secondly, command training establishes you as the pack leader of the house.

There are different ranks in a dog pack; alpha is the highest of those ranks. Alpha dogs are naturally and highly dominant over the other dogs in the pack. They are strong, high-spirited, calm, energetic and have a high prey drive.

If you fail to establish your dominance as the leader of the house, your Thai Ridgeback is sure to take this responsibility and stop paying heed to any of your commands. Hence, it is essential to let your dog know that it should obey you and not the other way around. Command training coupled with obedience training makes this possible.

How To Teach The Five Basic Commands Without Using Treats

Here are the five basic and important commands you need to teach your Thai Ridgeback to ensure it listens to you, obeys your commands, respects you, and follows your lead.

The Sit Command

The sit command is the most important dog obedience command; you simply must teach your Thai Ridgeback this command.

How to Teach Your Dog the Sit Command

To teach your Thai Ridgeback the sit command, hold a toy or anything your dog likes close to the dog's nose. Gradually, raise your hand so your dog follows it and lowers his or her bottom. The instant the dog gets into a sitting position, calmly say 'sit', give the dog the toy, and offer some affection as a reward. Repeat these steps a couple of times daily until your pup masters them.

Then ask your pup to sit every time before you give food, when going out for a walk, and in other situations where you want your dog to remain seated and calm.

The Come Command

This command helps your Thai Ridgeback come back to you in case you lose your grip on the leash when out for a walk, when you want your dog to enter a crate, or when you are training your dog to relieve itself in a safe spot.

How to Teach your Dog the Come Command

To practice this command, place a collar and leash on your Thai Ridgeback. Say 'come' and pull gently on the leash. As your dog comes towards you, praise and shower affection on him or her. After perfecting this command with the leash, get rid of the leash and practice the command in an enclosed, safe spot.

The Down Command

This command teaches your Thai Ridgeback to attain a submissive posture, something dogs are not very comfortable with; therefore, teach this command only when you are completely relaxed and can project an assertive and peaceful energy when doing it.

How to Teach the Down Command

To teach your Thai Ridgeback the down command, find something your dog likes a lot; this could be a favorite toy or object that is not food. Hold that object close to your dog's snout.

When your dog sniffs the object, move your hand down to the ground so your dog follows your movement. Slide the object in your hand along the ground right in front of your dog and encourage your dog to move his or her body in the direction of the toy (which is down).

When your dog is in the down pose, say 'down' and then offer the object of his or her desire and some much deserved affection. Repeat this daily and if your pup lunges upwards, say 'no' and then move your hand away. Never push your dog into a downward position; simply let your dog follow the steps in his or her own comfortable pace.

The Stay Command

Practice this command only after your Thai Ridgeback masters the sit command.

How to Teach the Stay Command

To teach the stay command, ask your Thai Ridgeback to sit first, then open your hand like a stop signal and gently say, 'stay'. Reward this behavior by giving praise and saying 'good dog'. To further develop this command, increase the space between you and your four-legged friend and again reward the proper behavior with praise.

It will take your dog a few days to master this command because self-control does not come easy to most dogs; nevertheless, the persistence and patience you show will surely pay off.

The Leave It Command

The leave it command is a very useful command because once your Thai Ridgeback learns it, it helps the dog stay away from unsafe things that may cause the dog harm, and teaches your dog to leave things when it intends to soil them.

How to Teach the Leave It Command

To teach this command, take your dog's favorite toys, one in each hand. Show your dog one fist with the toy inside it. Say 'leave it' and let your dog sniff, lick, paw, and do everything to get the toy. Ignore these behaviors.

When your dog stops trying, offer the toy in your other hand. Repeat this sequence until your pup moves far away from the first fist upon hearing you say 'leave it'. Give your pup the toy when it moves away from your first fist and looks at you. Practice this command daily until your dog perfects it.

These commands will come in handy when practicing different trainings.

Most Common Behavioral Issues and Problems

You have a puppy. Let's face it, there will be a lot of naughtiness around your house, and that is all normal. Puppies have a lot to learn on their way to becoming adult dogs, and that includes testing your limits and pushing the boundaries to see how far you will actually let them go.

Bad behavior is part of the deal of adopting a puppy. You should be aware that it is in your puppy's nature to show over excitement in ways you find unacceptable. Just like it is a natural thing to be stressed. It is your job to pin-point the reason for the bad behavior, eradicate the culprit, and completely redirect your puppy with nothing but love and understanding.

Correcting behavioral problems requires time and patience, but approaching the issue with an exaggerated reaction can set both you and your Thai Ridgeback to a path that is much harder to come back from.

Barking

You will find that an excessive amount of barking is going to be a really frustrating behavioral issue that you, as a new owner of a Thai Ridgeback, will have to deal with. This is also one of the biggest stressors that come up with a dog and its owner. This is why it is so essential to solve the problem before it gets to a level that is too hard to control.

First, you need to be able to understand why the Ridgeback is barking so much in the first place. These are some of the reasons why your Thai Ridgeback may be barking so much:

1. To try and get your attention

2. Because he is uncertain or fearful about something.

3. He wants to be able to assert this own dominance over a passerby or another animal.

There are different steps that you will need to take based on what the Thai Ridgeback is barking at. If you find that the puppy is barking at you at this time, then it is because he wants to gain more control, or he want your attention. Whether your puppy wants to be with the rest of the pack or he need some more exercise or something else, this is a behavior that you need to correct right away. To make this work, follow the steps below:

1. If you notice that the Thai Ridgeback continues to bark, turn your back to him and continue to ignore him until he stops.

2. Have some patience here because the puppy is going to continue his barking, in some cases, for a long period of time.

3. Once the Thai Ridgeback does stop barking, no matter how long it took, you can turn around and give the puppy lots of praise, treats, and attention.

4. Any time that the puppy starts to bark at you, repeat this process until he stops barking. This lets him know that you will only give him attention if he is not barking.

5. If you can't get the puppy to stop barking, then it is time to take a break in the crate until he is all done.

In some cases, the Thai Ridgeback is going to bark at passersby and animals. This issue is sometimes embarrassing when you bring your dog in public, but some people may feel a bit afraid if they don't know your dog. Many times, the dog owner is going to reinforce this behavior by screaming at the puppy to stop. You need to shift up the way that you respond to the barking first to get him to listen.

Let's say that the Thai Ridgeback is barking when he looks at people or dogs through the window. Some of the steps that you are able to use in order to get the Thai Ridgeback to stop barking in this manner include:

1. Call the puppy's name in a positive manner so that he put his focus on you instead of the object of his attention outside.

2. The positive aspect of this is going to be the most vital thing that you can do, but it is often the hardest as well. You need to find a way to be more motivating to the puppy than what he sees outside.

3. Once the puppy does look over at you, reward him before refocusing his attention on something else that he likes, such as a bone or a toy, so he doesn't get distracted again and start barking.

Furthermore, it is possible that your Thai Ridgeback is going to start barking at some people and other animals when he is in public. You will not be able to demand that he listen to you in the same manner that you could when at home. But this also doesn't mean that you have to just let the Thai Ridgeback bark all day long while you are out in public or that you have to go home. When you have a puppy who is barking at people and other animals when he is out in public, some of the steps that you can take include:

1. If you have a puppy who is already barking, it is time to move far enough away from the focus of his bark so that he stops the barking. If you are aware of a stimulus that may cause the puppy to bark, try to start out far enough away so that he isn't going to bark at it to start with.

2. When the puppy is looking in the direction of the stimuli, call his name and do what it takes to redirect his focus back on you. When the puppy looks at you, give him a treat. This is going to help him to associate that stimulus with positivity.

3. As you get the Thai Ridgeback to self-control and calm down, see if you are able to move a bit closer to the stimuli. With each step, stop and redirect the puppy back to you, and get him to gain the self-control that you want.

   a. The degree you move is going to vary between each animal, so take your time and see what works for your Thai Ridgeback.

4. During this method, make sure that you are the one who is maintaining the control, not the Thai Ridgeback. Check on a regular basis that the Thai Ridgeback remains relaxed during this process.

5. If you move closer and your puppy starts to bark again, it is time to move further away and then work to focus his attention back onto you before trying again.

Begging

This is actually a behavior that dog owners often unwittingly encourage by feeding him 'just this once' or for a little bit of quiet. This can get especially problematic if you allow the dog to sit at the table or underneath it to collect scraps.

Here are few tips to deal with this:

1. Avoid paying attention to your Thai Ridgeback when you're eating. Send him to his bed or out of the room if he continues to beg.
2. Tell everyone in the home not to feed him, that he must only eat from the bowl.
3. If your dog will not behave during meal times, tether him to something or put him in his crate.
4. Use 'sit,' and 'leave' commands.

Do not send your Thai Ridgeback a terrible message that you then want to retract later on, the sooner you start ensuring this rule is in place, the less time you'll have to spend getting rid of the begging habit.

Whining

Puppy whining may be cute at first, 'til it never stops. Whining is ultimately your dog's way of asking for help. He needs or wants something and is trying to get that in any way that he can. He may have lost his toy under the couch. He may want attention, or he may be bored. If you hear your Thai Ridgeback whining, it would be a good idea to investigate to see if there is an easy solution. Whining makes sense if your dog needs to go out, is hungry, or needs help getting something. But, if there are no good reasons, he may be whining just to get your attention, and that is bad.

When you want to eliminate this sort of whining for your attention, then, what you are going to do is eliminate giving your attention to him. He will no longer have your attention when he whines at you. If he still does not stop whining, calmly tell your Thai Ridgeback to be quiet. Your dog may not stop right away, especially if you have not taught that as a command. In due course, you may have to sort of snap at your Thai Ridgeback—using a louder tone to make him feel like he was scolded for the whining—and then stop paying any attention to him at all.

Digging

Even though this is not really a behavior that is going to be bad for the puppy, it can be harmful to your yard, and this may be the reason that you stop it. Of course, most people don't want to look out in their yard and see a bunch of holes everywhere, so dealing with this problem right from the beginning can really help.

The first thing that we have to look here is some of the reasons that a dog is going to dig. Each dog will be a bit different, but mostly, a dog is going to dig because his breed has a genetic disposition to digging, he is using this to help him get his energy out, or he feels bored.

This is one of those times when it is best to be preventative to make sure the dog does not dig. Exercising and stimulating your Thai Ridgeback can help him to not get bored, and it gets all of that extra energy out so that he is not likely to dig in your yard any longer. A puppy who is exerting all of his energy by playing with his toys, chewing on bones, and getting out on walks is going to find that he doesn't need to go to the yard to dig some holes. If genetics are the problem, then there probably isn't much that you can do to prevent this issue. You just need to learn how to correct the behavior to get it to stop with your Thai Ridgeback puppy.

If it happens that you catch the Thai Ridgeback digging in your yard and you want to get him to stop, there are a few steps that you are able to take. Some of these steps include:

1. If you find that your dog is already digging in your yard, tell him "NO" in a firm manner and get him away and distracted from the hole.

    a. If you can, immediately redirect your Thai Ridgeback to an appropriate item he can exert his energy into, such as running around the yard or chewing on a bone.

2. If you find a new hole that you didn't catch your Thai Ridgeback digging, there is nothing that you should do about the behavior. You need to make sure that you catch him in the act.

    a. Remember that you are not able to discipline the puppy for something he did that you weren't able to catch him doing.

    b. Your puppy is not going to remember that he dug the hole, even if it was just a minute ago. Scolding the puppy later on is not going to do you any good because the puppy won't have any idea what you are scolding him for.

Counter-Surfing

When compensated, counter surfing might consume a lot of time to stop. If you can ensure that he never track down anything great there, then, he will possibly surrender at that point. Put your Thai Ridgeback in his box or train him on his mat to get his food ready. Teach the "leave it" order. Never feed your Thai Ridgeback pieces from the counter when planning food or tidying up.

Puppies are animals of habits, and changing habits requires loads of exertion for you to transform them. Your pet needs to get what you need him to do, yet it will require time and persistence to make your targets understood and guide your puppy away from undesirable practices to better ones.

Biting Or Nipping

Biting and nipping are common aspects of dog play, especially for puppies. Biting and nipping can result in a lot of problems, not to mention that it will endanger your kids during playtime with your dog.

Try to shift his behavior from mouthing and nipping to merely licking. When he nips you, don't try to withdraw as that will only excite him and cause him to nip you more. Any serious biting should be met with withdrawal of attention to make him stop.

1. Have a noise that you use to associate biting with pain and displeasure.

2. Have teething toys to exchange for your hand, or whatever else your pup is biting. This is to let him know what is and is not okay to bite.

3. Use a firm "no" and stop playing when he turns to biting, and when he stops, show him his teething toy.

Remember to never associate biting with positive response. Even when it's cute and funny, you don't want to laugh or praise, and you want to immediately stop the biting, letting your puppy know that it is not acceptable.

Chewing

Another problem that a lot of puppies will fall into is that they will start to chew on a lot of things that they shouldn't, several items that you do not permit and are not part of their chew toys. When you first bring a Thai Ridgeback puppy home, especially if he is only about eight weeks old, remember that he doesn't know what is and what is not allowed to chew on. You have to step up and teach him these rules. Sure, it is easy to get frustrated with the puppy when he chews on the wrong thing, but you have to be proactive and teach your puppy what is appropriate behavior, particularly when it comes to chewing.

While it may feel like the puppy is purposely being naughty and just had to go after your favorite pair of shoes, remember that there are a lot of reasons why the Thai Ridgeback is chewing in the first place. He is not trying to be naughty, and he is not trying to make life more difficult for you. Some of the reasons that your Thai Ridgeback puppy may be chewing on things include:

1. Puppies have a need that is instinctual that tells them to chew on things.

2. Chewing is a good outlet for most dogs when it is time to exert energy. Your dog could be chewing on a variety of items when he has a lot of energy that he needs to get rid of or when he feels a bit bored with his activities.

3. Similar to what we see with infants, dogs like to put objects into their mouths in the hopes of figuring out what the object is and what they should do with it.

4. Dogs will often chew when they are teething. This chewing method will be a good way for them to soothe their gums.

Your Thai Ridgeback is going to chew, and he needs to chew, no matter if he is a brand-new puppy or you have had him around for some time. You can't stop him from chewing, but you can control what he is allowed to do this with. You just need to pick out the right chew toys or items that you are going to give to the puppy and teach him what he can chew on and what he needs to avoid.

The good news is there are a few things that you are able to do in order to make sure the Thai Ridgeback is going to chew on the right items and that he won't start to chew on some of your favorite items or on anything that he shouldn't have his mouth on. Some of the rules that you can follow when it comes to this include:

1. Always have some approved chewing objects that you can give to your Thai Ridgeback. Your puppy is going to chew no matter what, so make sure that you provide him with some toys or objects that he is allowed to chew on instead of getting mad when he chews on items that you don't approve of.

2. Be strict with what he can chew on and what he can't chew on. From the start, you have to be strict on this and may have to keep the puppy confined to one area. But this is his learning period, and you are going to see the best results when you can keep track of the puppy and make sure that the he doesn't get ahold of things he shouldn't have.

3. Redirect the Thai Ridgeback to an object that you approve of for him to chew on. The puppy is sometimes going to get away from you and will try to chew on something that he should not. When you catch him in the act, don't try to shout or yell or get mad about it. This just encourages him because the puppy sees that he is getting attention from this. Instead, when you find him, say "NO" and then redirect him over to an item that is designed for him to chew on.

Leash Pulling

Another common issue that you will see when you bring home a new Thai Ridgeback puppy is that he likes to pull on the leash. This one seems to be a certainly tough problem for most dog owners to deal with, and it seems like most owners are going to allow their dog to pull on the leash forever. The good news is that it is possible to train your Thai Ridgeback puppy to stop pulling on the leash, making things a whole lot easier for you.

The bottom line to remember here is that your leash should never be tight when you try to take the Thai Ridgeback on a walk. A loose leash is going to be the standard that you set, and it means that there is a small part of slack on the leash between the Thai Ridgeback and you. There are some reasons why you would want this to happen. It is going to teach the puppy that you are the pack leader and he should respect you. You don't want the puppy to start to think that he gets to lead you all the time. When the Thai Ridgeback puppy decides to make the leash tight and pulls on it, it is going to add a ton of stress and pressure to the neck, and this can be harmful to him. Pulling can also cause some damage to your own joints on the arms and shoulders. And when the Thai Ridgeback puppy goes with a loose leash, it is going to become a much more enjoyable walk for both of you.

Now, this brings up the question of what you are supposed to do when the Thai Ridgeback decides to pull on the leash when you are walking. This may slow down your walk a bit, but you will find that most puppies are going to catch on quick, and doing this can truly make a difference in how well the walk goes. Taking some time now will help you have much more enjoyable walks overall. Some of the steps that you are able to do to help stop the Thai Ridgeback puppy from pulling on the leash will include:

1. Any time that you feel the Thai Ridgeback is getting excited and starts pulling on the leash, stop right where you are and don't go any further.

2. When the Thai Ridgeback starts to see that you have stopped and looks back at you, work with the clicker word.

3. Wait for the puppy to walk back to you, and when the puppy does this, reward him with a treat.

4. If you notice that the puppy is not coming back to you, lure him back using the heeling position and with a treat if you need it.

5. Now, there are some times when the Thai Ridgeback is still not going to come over to you. If this is the situation, you can take another step back. Continue to do this 'til the Thai Ridgeback starts to walk back to you.

6. Repeat this process persistently during the walk until the puppy learns that the leash needs to be loose.

As you can imagine, this will slow down the walk for a bit. You may only want to go on a walk down the block or so 'til the Thai Ridgeback starts to get the hang of what you are doing. The good news here is that the Thai Ridgeback will learn, and you will get the puppy to walk alongside you, with a nice loose leash rather than one that is tight and harming both you and your Thai Ridgeback puppy, in no time.

Chasing

If your dog is prone to chasing, that's a throwback to his genetic history as a predatory animal. All predators have the impulse to chase what is fleeing – it's the same reason your dog enjoys chasing a ball. But just because he's acting out of a natural instinct, that doesn't make chasing a good thing, or something you have to live with. Certainly, joggers, mailmen, and people on bicycles would appreciate it if you worked with your dog to rid him of this behavior.

Chasing may seem like a minor nuisance when your Thai Ridgeback is young and small. It's quite another matter when he's grown to be a big, heavy dog that can pose a serious threat. It's crucial to train your puppy not to chase people for any reason, and as with other training, it's best if you can start that training when the dog is very young.

Training Your Thai Ridgeback Not to Chase Others

You should not let your Thai Ridgeback off the leash until you know he doesn't chase, or until you've trained him not to. Letting him chase is dangerous to him and to others. It's irresponsible of you as an owner, is illegal, and could leave you in a position in which you are liable for being sued.

So, train your p Thai Ridgeback in a controlled area, like a fenced-in yard, and make sure he isn't prone to chasing before you risk him getting free. If he is prone to chasing, you'll need to choose training areas where he won't be distracted by people or animals he'd like to chase. You need him to focus when you are training him, so he can more quickly understand the behavior you want from him. You will be asking him to perform commands over and over again to reach a place where he responds in the correct way, automatically. A distraction – such as something his instinct tells him to chase – pulls his focus away, and slows the training down.

So, hold any training sessions away from the temptation to chase, but in particular, hold training about not chasing indoors, in your home, to ensure he won't be distracted. Put him on leash and stand with him at the end of a hallway, or the edge of a room. Wave a tennis ball in front of your puppy, but don't let him touch the ball. Then, roll the ball across the room, or to the end of the hallway, giving the command "Off" to tell your puppy he is not to chase after the ball. If he starts to go after the ball, give him the command "Off" once again, and tug the leash firmly.

During this training, make certain your Thai Ridgeback does not touch the ball. If he reaches it, he may be confused into thinking that the "Off" command means "Go get the ball!" By repeating this exercise for a number of times, your Thai Ridgeback will learn what you mean by the "Off" command. Of course, when your puppy figures it out and responds in the way you want by not chasing down the ball, praise him to the skies and reward him with a special treat.

At that point, repeat the exercise a few times to make absolutely certain your Thai Ridgeback understands, praising each time he performs well. Then move to another area of the house and do the exercise again. When your puppy obeys the "Off" command in several areas of your house, try the same exercise off-leash – but still only work with him while inside your house, or from within a fenced-in yard. Give your puppy all the time he needs to learn not to chase; the instinct to chase may be strong in him, and rushing the process will only slow his learning down in the long run. It's also important not to rush the training because to do so is to take the risk he'll chase another animal or a person, and not have been trained in a way that gives you any control over him.

When you think he's fully ready, test your puppy's ability to resist chasing out in the "real" world. To test him, get help from a friend who is willing to pose as a jogger. It's better if the friend is someone your puppy has never seen before – he needs to believe this "jogger" is a stranger. Stand near the street, holding your puppy on a leash. When the friend comes jogging by, give the "Off" command. Your puppy should not move toward the jogger in any way. If he does, firmly tug on the leash; if he performs well, praise and reward him.

Training Your Thai Ridgeback Not to Chase Cars

If your Thai Ridgeback chases people or other dogs, he is more likely a threat to them than they are to him. But if he chases cars, he is the one most likely to be hurt, possibly fatally. As early as possible in his life, train your puppy to understand that chasing cars is never, ever acceptable. A puppy that chases a car may one day be a puppy that catches a car, and nothing good will come of that.

Dogs chase cars for a number of reasons. First, there's the hunting instinct to chase what moves. That's an ingrained behavior, instinctual to some dogs, particularly those from hunting or herding breeds. A dog that's from a hunting breed experiences a thrill when he engages in a chase. A herding dog is instinctively trying to control which direction a moving car moves in, but just because the behavior is instinctual, that doesn't make it desirable in any way. Much of the training you've done with your Thai Ridgeback has been to work with him to overcome his instinctual response, and this training is no exception. Understand that he is responding based on instinct, and he isn't deliberately disobeying you when he chases a car; but even so, it's important that you train him to obey your commands.

Your Thai Ridgeback may be drawn to chase cars not out of defensiveness, but out of joy; many dogs associate cars with fun trips with you. Most dogs love to ride in the car, and some puppy behaviorists believe they chase cars hoping to get a ride.

But it doesn't matter why your Thai Ridgeback chases cars, because whatever his reason, it's imperative that you put a stop to this dangerous activity as soon as you can. The "Off" command is the basis of training your puppy not to chase cars. It's a powerful command with a number of uses and should be thoroughly understood and obeyed by every puppy.

With the "Off" command, you are instructing your Thai Ridgeback to stay where he is – no matter how interested or excited he is by a passing dog, jogger, bicyclist or car. Training your puppy not to chase cars involves "distraction training."

For this training, put your puppy's leash and collar on him. You'll need the help of at least one other person (the "distraction"). This training volunteer will slowly drive by, in front of your Thai Ridgeback, luring him into a chase. It's really best if the volunteer drives your car, as dogs can distinguish one car from another, and yours is particularly appealing – especially if that's the car your Thai Ridgeback is used to being in when he goes for rides.

As your friend drives by, watch carefully to see how your puppy reacts. If he moves at all, whether a small movement or a jump or lunge, give the "Off" command and immediately return him to the sitting position. If he stays put, let him know he did exactly what you wanted by praising him and giving him something tasty.

Repeat this training several times over the course of the next several days. As your Thai Ridgeback begins to obey you, move to the next level of the training by standing further away from your puppy for the test. You can easily accomplish this with a retractable leash, lengthened to put your puppy further away from you. At each stage, when your puppy is fully obeying the "Off" command, lengthen the distance more, but always make sure you retain control.

You may think the goal of this training is to allow you to have your Thai Ridgeback outside, off-leash, safely, but your puppy is never entirely safe if he is outside and off-leash. The training to prevent him from chasing cars, other animals, or people is just to give you an extra safety measure, in case you ever have him outside and off-leash – which, again, you should never do. Always have him on his leash, or supervised, or, best of all, both. Remember – dogs can be unpredictable, especially when tempted. Ensure your puppy is trained in the "Off" command, in case his chase instinct kicks in and you need to get control of him so he and others are safe.

Urine Marking

You will also experience dogs that tend to mark their sent by urinating on different parts of the house. Puppies typically do this on vertical objects such as the legs of a chair or a piece of furniture. This usually happens when your puppy is around 5 months all the way up to 2 years.

Puppies that have not yet been neutered will usually have this kind of behavior although you also spot neutered dogs that do the same. Dogs usually scent mark because they are either excited or anxious when they spot the presence of another dog. Sometimes they just do it as a habit.

Dogs typically scent mark outside the house. If you happen to have new pets however dogs might usually mark parts of the house. If you happen to be new to a household, dolls will also have this tendency.

If you encounter this, make sure to rule out any underlying medical conditions first by paying a visit to your local veterinarian. You can also talk to him about neutering your Thai Ridgeback however you always need to prioritize the training first and see if you can train your dog out of this habit.

Don't punish your p Thai Ridgeback if he marks your house and you always need to clean up the mess with your enzyme based detergent or cleaner.

You can take some steps to limit your puppy's access to your house. Always pay attention to his behavior and look for those signs when your dog is thinking about scent marking an area. You'll usually notice that he tends to circle around and sniff a particular area. This should be a pretty good sign that you need to prevent that behavior by bringing your dog outside right away.

You can also spend more time walking you Thai Ridgeback. If it seems that your dog is reacting to a new situation such as having a new pet or person in your home, you can work with your puppy to build a good relationship with them. If you have a new friend for example, you might want to have your dog spend time playing with him or her.

Dealing With Separation Anxiety

The one thing that puppies hate and would rather befriend a cat is being alone. They are more social than us, and the pack means a lot to them. It can make them anxious knowing that its pack is not near it. If you allow them, or they get the chance they would like nothing better than to follow you around the house, to the store, to your work which is a train journey away. As much as you would like to spend all your time with them, it is very much realistic to say that you might have to leave them for a while almost everywhere. Although it is not the simplest thing to spot - the separation anxiety; you might hear them whining in a sad fashion when you leave but that does not necessarily have to be anxiety. So, the primary step of dealing with this separation anxiety and making this relationship easier for both of you, we must try to understand how to determine if the pup is anxious or not.

Mostly, signs of anxiety in dogs can be noticed in their behavioral anomalies compared to normal times. It can be that when you leave the house, the puppy goes on to destructively chew things hurting themselves and spoiling the toy or the sofa you asked them not to chew. It might also be possible that due to anxiousness, it could lose bladder control and then might urinate or even defecate in the house, even though he or she is potty trained to perfection. Or your pup could resonate with excessive digging hurting their paws in the end to calm their anxiousness. All this could be hard evidence to the fact that your pooch is having separation anxiety.

Such behavior is completely normal, and usually happens when the dog is living a life where there are long periods of separation and there is not much human interaction. For your aid, here are certain tips and steps which you can do in order to help your Thai Ridgeback go through this period and ultimately solve this.

- It does sound quite intuitive to leave the house in a rather grand fashion with respect to the feelings of the dog. Basically, what we are trying to say - that when you leave the house by giving the puppy a lot of petting, it gets super into you and is loving you all it can but at that moment if you leave the house and do not return for hours; it would rather feel like it has done something wrong or simply be sad upon this separation.

- Now you need to make your pup realize that you will be coming home, because the reason that it is so sad and anxious is that in doggy time it has almost been days since you have returned. Therefore, it becomes essential to tell the dog something it can associate with you coming back - say Goodbye or an equivalent.

- Animals easily sleep when it is dark and therefore before you go make sure its sleeping area or the crate is kept in the dark and is comfortable for the dog.

- Again, the importance of good, squeaky toys cannot be undermined as it is always a good idea to leave them with toys when leaving so that they can spend time chewing and being engaged rather than stress chewing which might not be on toys but on off limited stuff of your household.

- A good idea for you would be to leave something in their sleeping place that can smell of you, like a sock or a worn-out soft piece of clothing. This would make them more aware of your presence and offer reassurance like none other.

- Now, the important point here is that puppies that have serious separation anxiety are also at the same time very sensitive puppy - which means that you shouting at them could be associated with anything but the destruction they caused as the destruction is a result of panic but not something they wanted to do willingly. So let us say you come back home to find things out of place, do not shout at the pup or it will be associated with your arrival.

- If the above methods do not work, it is best to go to your Vet and ask for help and consultation. Or also it would not be one of the worst ideas, to try a dog walker because it you are gone for really long hours, you need to have a certain companion with the dog.

You should not be disheartened or very sad at this in terms of training. This is so because anxiety and good behavior are not related on a fundamental level. Anxiety is a situation of distress where the mind resorts to certain subconscious methods of dealing. In this situation, the conscious part of the dog's brain that is developed through training is not in use and henceforth there is not much to train also when it comes to dealing with separation anxiety.

Physical Exercises

Staying fit and healthy requires regular exercise. This is also true for dogs. They warrant physical activity to stay healthy. Often, we forget to exercise our dogs because life gets so busy.

How Much Exercise Do Dogs Need?

As a general rule, dogs should exercise one to two hours per day to stay healthy. Depending on your dog's age, breed, and tolerance, they may need more or less. Shih Tzus may want to lounge on the couch, while Border Collies, Thai Ridgebacks, or Bluetick Coonhounds may perform agility for four hours every day and still want more. Finding your dog's exercise requirements may take some trial and error, as no two dogs are alike. You should give your dog as much exercise as it wants, but take it slow.

If you're starting a new exercise program for your Thai Ridgeback, make sure to start slowly and let your dog build up endurance and tolerance to the exercise. Look out for signs of exhaustion; they may include heavy panting, lameness, wheezing, disorientation, and slowing or stopping to lie down during activities. Don't let your Thai Ridgeback out on hot days unless it has access to fresh, cool water. Your dog may appear tired, achy, or disinterested in exercise if he or she is tired, achy, or disinterested in exercise. Call your vet if you spot any signs of illness while exercising.

What's the Best Exercise for My Thai Ridgeback?

Exercise and your Thai Ridgeback can go hand in hand with several activities. Although some activities provide your dog with more exercise than you, they're still fun. Walk your dog to a dog park, or play fetch with a ball. Have you thought about participating in dog sports with your dog? Competitions in agility, catch, and herding are great places to begin.

Let's start something fun and introduce a new type of exercise to your Thai Ridgeback. While keeping your dog healthy, it's a wonderful way to bond.

Taking a walk

We tend to give our dogs walks as the classic form of exercise. It's okay, though. Most dogs love walking!

A walk is a wonderful way for your Thai Ridgeback to explore the world with her nose in addition to getting some exercise. Take your time. Your dog can explore as much as he or she likes on the walk. Make sure your dog sees and smells something new now and then by taking a different route.

Running

Some dogs enjoy running as an exercise. Not all dogs can indeed tolerate this type of exercise, but it's a necessity for some!

Using a hands-free leash can make running with your Thai Ridgeback easier. Safety and legal considerations make off-leash running unwise. Nevertheless, it might be considered if your dog has a truly reliable recall and local laws allow dog's off-leash.

Start slowly; then kick up your speed and distance when running with your dog. Hot asphalt can burn your paws, so avoid running in high temperatures. Check in regularly with your dog to monitor its exercise tolerance and ensure that it's getting the necessary breaks. Bring plenty of water along on runs.

Cycling

Some dogs aren't built to run alongside your bike. This can pose a risk to both you and your pet. It can still be fun to ride a bike with your Thai Ridgeback if you do it correctly. It would be best if you started slowly. Make sure your dog gets used to the bike. Continue running and keep up with her as she gets used to it. It's helpful if you rode slowly at first, avoiding a lot of turns and twists. It's also useful if you always keep your dog on a leash, so consider getting a bicycle attachment so that you won't need to hold the leash.

Hiking

A hike with your Thai Ridgeback might be the perfect activity for someone who loves nature and dogs. A hike will give your dog a deeper experience of the world than a simple walk. Start out with short hikes on a cooler day when hiking with your dog for the first time. Once your dog has gotten used to easy to moderate hikes and will be more sure-footed, avoid difficult trails.

Ensure that you bring a lot of water. It's even possible for your dog to take its own backpack; make sure it's well-balanced and not too heavy.

Swimming

Not all dogs are capable of swimming, contrary to popular belief. Some dogs dislike swimming. Anyone who has a water dog knows this. Take your dog swimming! You can combine swimming with the game of fetch to make it even more fun. Just be sure to follow these water safety guidelines.

You can still teach your Thai Ridgeback to swim if the pup likes the water but cannot swim. Begin with shallow water and a doggie life jacket until it gets the hang of it. If the fur baby likes the water, then it'll likely get comfortable real quick. Don't push the dog into the water if it doesn't like it. It may just be that your dog loves the land!

Games

You can play many fun games with your Thai Ridgeback, some of which will also provide some exercise. Dogs get moderate exercise from fetch, hide-and-seek, and tug of war while you get light exercise from them.

It's also possible to use games to train your dog, which is a great way to stimulate his mind.

Dog Sports

Nowadays, there are many exciting dog sports available, and new ones are always popping up. Agility and canine freestyle will give your Thai Ridgeback a great workout and offer some light to moderate exercise for you.

Make sure you research the dog sports that might be right for your Thai Ridgeback before you get started. After that, look for classes that will teach you and your dog the sport in your area.

Safety First

Please consult your veterinarian before beginning any exercise program for your dog. Let your dog set the pace when exercising with her. Take water and rest breaks from time to time. Dogs with short muzzle, such as a Bulldog or Pug, should avoid exercising in hot temperatures.

Whatever type of dog you have, be on the lookout for signs of exhaustion, illness, or injury. Don't exercise if your pet seems tired or ill. When exercising with your dog, pay attention to your surroundings. It may be dangerous for your dog to be distracted if other dogs or people are around, especially if it's is off-leash.

Dog Walking

Before you go for a walk, you'll need a leash. At the market you will find various kinds available. It's important to get a lead that that offers good control over your dog, especially when you are training a puppy. Retractable slip leads are very trendy these days. The slip lead is a single-piece lead with an O-ring at the end that is opposite to the handle. It will tighten around the dog if she pulls too hard. These slip leads are also known as British style lead, and they are often used in training or the show ring.

You will need to walk your dog regularly. According to experts, there are plenty of benefits that come with it, for both you and the dog.

- **Bond strengthening.** Since you will be alone with your pet, you will have quality time together. Experts report that this time is vital in forming a deep and trusting relationship with your dog. The time that you spend together with him also plays a vital role in his behavioral development, as you will know what habits he is developing, and can work to correct any bad ones.

- **Weight control.** Just like humans, dogs are bound to gain a lot of weight when they lead a sedentary lifestyle. If you live in an apartment, your four-legged friend has little space to exercise; therefore, he gains weight. During the walk, he burns calories hence bringing about weight loss. And it'll do you some good, too!

- **Better mental well-being.** If you exercise regularly, you can bear witness that you feel much better afterward. This is because your body discharges hormones that enhance your mental well-being. This is the same for your dog. When he exercises, he feels better about himself, thus becoming a more relaxed companion.

- **More exposure**. When you walk your dog, you expose him to new people, experiences, and settings. This helps him to learn new things which are crucial for growth.

- **Decrease loneliness.** If you live alone, and work outside the house, this means your dog spends most of his time alone. Just like humans, dogs are social beings. When you are walking him, you give him company which helps him feel loved and valued.

- **Longer life.** Since dogs who exercise are fitter and healthier, they tend to live longer. Since they have longer lives, you enjoy the company of your Thai Ridgeback for a longer time.

How To Walk Your Dog

While many people know that they need to walk their dogs, studies show that few dog owners know how to do it properly. To help you out, here are tips on how to properly walk your Thai Ridgeback:

- **Always keep him on a leash.** When your dog is on a leash you have full control of him, and you are the one in charge of the walk – not the dog. The best way to holding the leash is to wrap it around your hand so there is little space between you and him.

- **Treat him.** It's always recommended that you train your Thai Ridgeback during the walk. Some of the things you can work on are walking, sitting, and when to pull on the leash. When he behaves the way you want, you should reward him with his favorite treat.

- **Make the walk comfortable.** Make sure the leash is made from a comfortable material, and that you apply gentle pressure. Remember the walk is meant to be fun. Also, the time of day that you walk him determines how comfortable the dog will be. For instance, you might avoid walking him at noon on hot days.

Chapter Seven: Vet Care for Your Thai Ridgeback

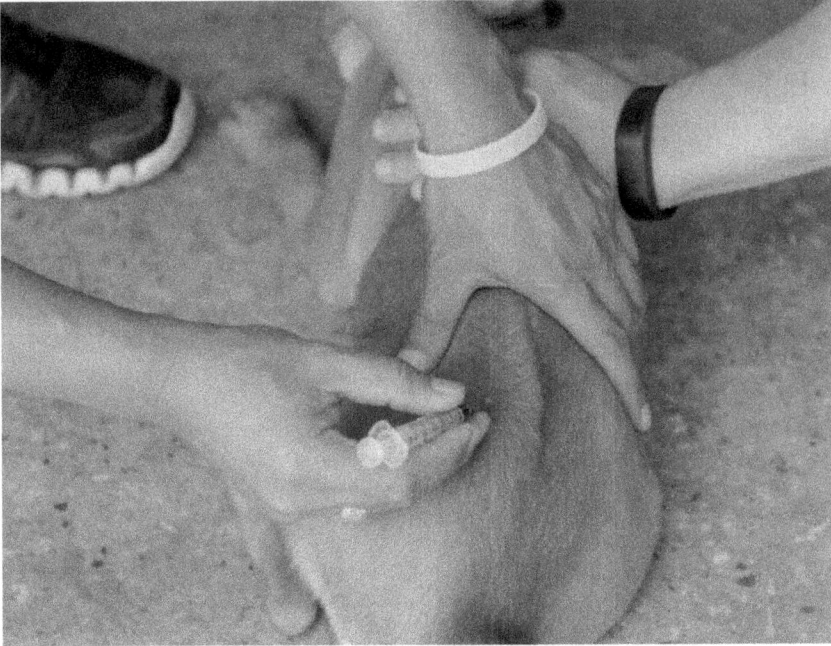

Vaccinations

Vaccinations must be performed on a regular basis by pet owners, and dogs must be vaccinated at the right period. This helps to strengthen the animal's resistance to certain infections that regularly cause difficulties in dogs. Dogs who are orphaned owing to the loss of their mother have a weaker immune system. These animals must be specially safeguarded against a variety of illnesses.

Vaccination is often initiated around the age of five to six weeks, and previous to this age, maternal immunity aids the animal in developing natural disease resistance. It is always preferable to deworm the animal before to immunization, and this is frequently emphasized. Puppies are frequently afflicted by parvo viral infections, hence vaccination against the virus is done at a young age. The booster dosage for each vaccination must be administered at the proper time, which aids in the development of an appreciable immune status. Many nations have rabies vaccination programs in place.

As a result, rabies vaccination is always emphasized. Rabies tags are even attached to the dog collars of the majority of the canines. Rabies vaccination is administered between the ages of thirteen and fifteen weeks, and it is administered again at the age of fifteen months. This is dependent on the type of vaccination given. This happens every three years.

Give measles virus vaccination and killed parvovirus vaccine to dogs that have not had colostrum's or dogs in high-risk locations before five weeks of age. The Leptospira serovar vaccination is administered at six to eight weeks of age, tenth to twelfth weeks, and thirteenth to sixteenth weeks.

Then, every year, repeat this process. In the case of dogs, Bordetella and Lyme disease immunizations are solely elective. Vaccinations against canine parainfluenza, canine parvovirus, and canine adenovirus type two are administered on a regimen identical to that used for leptospiral serovars.

Symptoms of Illness

The most essential indicators of your Thai Ridgeback dog's health are symptoms of illness. For example, if the dog has continuous nasal discharge, it signals nasal congestion, and if the discharge is heavy, the dog may have pneumonia.

If the Thai Ridgeback dog vomits once or twice, this may not be considered a major indicator of illness; but, if the dog continues to vomit, this is something that should be investigated.

If the Thai Ridgeback dog is constantly itching, it is necessary to examine the dog closely and examine the skin by separating the hair material. You may also see a large number of ticks or lice on the skin, which may appear normal from a distance.

If the dog passes loose stool once or twice, this is not cause for concern; but, if the dog passes loose stool on a regular basis, the dog is thought to have digestive issues. If the dog does not pass stool for two to three days, digestive disturbances must be thoroughly ruled out.

Simply study the dog's walking movements with patience and rule out any aberrant movements in the dog. If the dog limps, he or she may have foot lesions. Similarly, if the elderly dog is hesitant to move and consumes less food, as well as vomiting on a regular basis, acute renal illnesses such as nephritis must be ruled out.

If you see whiteness in your eyes, it might be due to a corneal opacity caused by a condition like trypanosomiasis. When a dog gets anemic, the mucous membrane of the eyes becomes paler, and in extreme cases, the mucous membrane may turn white. If the dog bites the chain, the owners, or anybody else, look for behavioral issues, and rabies must be ruled out.

Neutering/Spaying

If you are a first-time dog owner, you might be wondering if you need to spay/neuter your Thai Ridgeback dog. The answer is 100% absolutely. Not only will this prevent numerous medical issues for your dog, but it also helps reduce overpopulation which is a huge problem in many cities all over the world. Every year, millions of dogs are euthanized because shelters don't have the resources of space to care for that many animals. By making sure to neuter/spay your dog, you are playing your part to prevent this tragic problem.

What exactly is the difference between neutering and spaying? It's quite simple actually, male dogs get neutered and female dogs get spayed. We will discuss the must-knows of each process below.

Neutering Your Male Dog

Neutering is actually a very simple surgery that sterilizes a male dog so he cannot parent puppies. Neutering also lowers the risk of certain diseases, unwanted behaviors, and socialization problems. The neutering surgery is simpler than the spaying surgery. The veterinarian will put the dog under using anesthesia and make a small incision in the front of the dog's scrotum. The veterinarian will then cut the stalks of the testicle and then remove it through the incision. Most likely the incision will need stitches and the dog will have to wear a 'cone collar' during its recovery to prevent licking or nibbling of the area. In just two short weeks the incision would heal and the dog goes back to their normal life.

Besides not having the ability to conceive any puppies there are many more reasons to neuter your dog. First of all, they are less likely to get diseases such as testicular cancer or prostate diseases. Due to having less testosterone in the dog's system, they will likely be calmer. In addition, dogs naturally mark their territory using their urine. Since they have less testosterone, your dog will naturally mark less. The lower level of testosterone should improve behaviors like aggression and humping. Although it is a myth that your dog will stop humping after being neutered, dogs still mount and hump to exert dominance and not solely just to mate. It is less likely that your dog will get into fewer fights with other male dogs.

Male dogs can get neutered any time after two months of age. Veterinarians normally advise waiting until doggy puberty hits at six months but it is a case-by-case scenario. Talk to your veterinarian to get the best recommendation for your specific dog breed. Dogs that get neutered before puberty (6 months) typically grow a bit bigger compared to those that are neutered after puberty because of the testosterone involved in bone growth. Depending on the owner more growth may be more or less desirable. Keep in mind that most dogs are sexually mature by the fifth or sixth month so make the necessary preparations to have your dog neutered around that age.

The normal procedure of the neutering surgery starts with pre-surgical bloodwork for your dog. This is to make sure that your dog is healthy enough for surgery and doesn't have any preexisting conditions that may affect the anesthesia or surgery itself. More often than not, young dogs are healthy and won't have any issues but it is still a step that is needed to get a reference for future bloodwork. Your dog should not eat for 8 hours before the surgery as the anesthesia may cause nausea.

The neutering surgery is typically very simple and straightforward. The harder part, however, is the post-surgery care for your dog. Here are a few things to keep in mind after your dog gets neutered:

- Male dogs/puppies usually are allowed to go home the same day after the surgery
- Your dog may have some nausea and not eat for a day or two. No need to worry as your dog will be fine if he misses a few meals. He will eat again once nausea fades.
- The first few days after the surgery you may notice that your dog's scrotum is swollen. This is not harmful but just be sure that your dog cannot lick or irritate the incision. A lot of the times the swelling gets worse if your dog got access to the wound. By making your dog wear the "cone of shame" they will be unable to reach their scrotum area.

- Depending on what kind of stitches your veterinarian used, they may need to be removed after a week or two. Some will use self-dissolving stitches that will go away on its own.
- Try to restrict your dog's activity after the surgery if they are playful. Try to make sure they are playing gently to prevent the incision from opening up.
- Some bruising may occur near the incision, this is normal.

Keep an eye out on your dog's incision to see if there is any discharge or if your dog is in excessive pain. It is rare for a dog to feel this much pain after this surgery but it is possible. Contact your veterinarian if you see any unusual symptoms or behaviors in your dog. Your dog may not be his usual self right after the surgery but give him a few days to recover before you begin to worry.

Spaying Your Female Dog

The spay surgery prevents female dogs from being able to get pregnant by removing the ovaries and uterus. It is otherwise known as getting your dog "fixed". This surgery is not as simple as the neuter surgery, it is a major surgery and your Thai Ridgeback may be affected for up to a few weeks.

However, she will enjoy numerous health benefits and you won't have to worry about her being in heat.

Some dog owners think that they can easily prevent pregnancy just by keeping their dogs inside or in a secure yard away from male dogs. However, even experienced dog owners may have a surprise "oops"! Dogs can jump over or dig under gates to mate. When two dogs with raging hormones are near each other at the wrong time, you may have an accidental pregnancy.

The main benefit of spaying your Thai Ridgeback dog is to prevent unwanted pregnancies that may contribute to overpopulation. Like we mentioned earlier, millions of dogs are euthanized every year due to overpopulation in shelters. Besides this reason, there are several other benefits to spaying your dog.

- Getting your Thai Ridgeback dog spayed reduces risk of certain illnesses such as mammary gland cancer and pyometra (a common infection of the uterus that is life-threatening)
- Getting your dog spayed helps prevent males from being wildly attracted to your dog when in heat
- Getting your dog spayed prevents her from having her period so you don't need to use sanitary pads or have a mess all over your home.

- Spaying eliminates a terrible odor that your dog releases when in heat. Although your nose is not as sensitive as a dog's, humans are still able to smell this distinct odor.

Female dogs go into heat once every eight months or so and lasts up to three weeks at a time. They also don't go through menopause and will regularly be in heat for their entire lives until they are spayed. So, when is the best time to spay your dog? A veterinarian will be able to make a recommendation based on your dog's breed and needs. Most female dogs have this surgery after 2 months and before their first heat (6 - 7 months). Some veterinarians will recommend the spaying surgery right before the first heat so they could tolerate the necessary anesthesia. A larger and more fully grown dog is more difficult to spay than a smaller dog which is why veterinarians will give their recommendation on a case-by-case basis.

Even if your Thai Ridgeback dog is given a balanced diet and an environment that encourages good health, there are still some health issues that can occur. Knowing the potential health issues that this breed is susceptible to will allow you to spot them early and provide the appropriate treatment.

Parasites Worms And Common Illnesses

This section focuses on parasites and other common conditions that could affect your Thai Ridgeback. This section is essential as you need to be aware of parasites and common conditions that can affect your Thai Ridgeback and how to treat them.

Parasitic Worms

Parasites are a major concern in the digestive system. Internal parasites, also known as worms, can cause serious health problems for Thai Ridgeback dogs and Thai Ridgeback puppy.

Roundworms

Roundworm is the most common type of worm. However, there are many variations. Roundworm infections can cause itching in the anus, worms in dogs' feces, and loss of condition.

Mother dogs can transmit roundworms to their puppies. All Thai Ridgeback puppies will be properly wormed by the breeder before being sent to their new homes.

While some worms are not symptomatic, others can cause serious health problems for Thai Ridgeback dogs.

Whipworm and hookworm are roundworms that can cause digestive problems in dogs. Hookworm grasps onto the stomach wall, causing severe and constant discomfort for the dog.

Dogs can be affected by a roundworm infestation in their digestive system. However, roundworm larvae have far greater dangers. Roundworms can be transmitted between species by being a zoonotic parasite. Roundworm larvae can be ingested by people and become confused inside the body, leading to blindness. Blindness is the goal for roundworm larvae.

Tapeworms

Tapeworms are parasites that can live in your dog's intestines. They can also grow to large sizes throughout the intestinal tract. Tapeworms reproduce by shedding a portion of their long, segmented bodies. This is done with the feces and drops from the anus. Tapeworms are happy to live in both dogs' and humans' digestive systems. The main problem is that the tapeworm will eat a lot of food and grow. Your dog will be starved and not getting enough nutrients.

The best way to keep your chances of getting infected under control is to use basic worming tablets. These should be taken every three months. Make sure you give your Thai Ridgeback the right dosage. The kilo of your dog is usually used to determine the correct dosage. Be aware that different brands may suggest different numbers of tablets. This could be due to the size and/or potency of each tablet.

Lungworms/Heartworms

The lungworm/heartworm is another type of worm that can have serious consequences.

When the larvae of this type of worm gets into an animal's body, it migrates to the heart or lung. As shown above, it quickly reproduces to infest the major organ. The damage to the heart and lungs is already well-established by the time you notice symptoms.

The symptoms include excessive coughing, loss of heart and lung function, and even loss of consciousness. This parasite is now more common and being detected in areas that have never seen it before.

This parasite's larvae can enter the body through a mosquito bite, or by ingestion. Lungworm infestations are more common in dogs that eat snails, slugs and eggs.

Preventative medicine has evolved with rapid spreading infections. If you live in an area at high risk of infection, consult your veterinarian to discuss preventive measures.

It is a good idea to consult your vet about the possible types of worms that your dog might be susceptible to. These worming tablets can be purchased at pet shops and general stores. Remember to choose the right type of worming tablet for your dog's size and age.

External Parasites– Fleas And Other Suckers

External parasites are another type of parasite that could potentially impact your Thai Ridgeback dog.

Fleas

Fleas are clever little jumpers that can jump up to half a meter, and often jump onto dark areas. Fleas are likely to jump on dogs who walk past them.

The female flea will lay eggs as soon as she has found her host. She can leave 800 eggs in your home and on your dog's skin in a matter of months. Fleas can wait months for eggs to hatch, so it is important that spring is when they are most active. Flea symptoms include a profusion itchy bite and grit like dirt that turns yellow in water.

As a preventative measure, many vets will recommend that you apply chemical treatment every few months. This usually takes the form of a spot treatment that is applied to the neck of the dog.

Holistic veterinarians recommend that dogs only require chemical treatment in cases of actual infestation. I tend to agree with this. This logic is to make sure that the dog is not exposed to chemicals unless absolutely necessary. If your dog does not seem to be under constant attack during the summer months, you can apply for treatment only when you feel the symptoms are present and not every day.

You can keep your Thai Ridgeback happy and healthy by feeding him well, cleaning him with a lemon juice/vinegar solution, and then rinsing him in it once a week. This will keep fleas away.

Essential oils like lemongrass, lemongrass and citronella are also favorites of mine. These oils can be used as natural flea/tick killers. There's been much discussion on the internet. You can also find interesting videos from YouTube users sharing their favorite remedies.

Ticks

Ticks are another type of parasite. They don't live with dogs, but rather wander onto them to feed and then disappear when they are full.

An empty tick searching for food (blood), is no bigger than a pin's head, but can expand to look like a small pea. Once it has found a spot on the dog's body, the tick will dive in and soak as much blood as possible. You will find them on the dog bed, in the crate or on the floor.

Ticks are not distinguishable and will happily bite humans, cattle, sheep, deer, and dogs. They are most active in the summer months. However, they can be found in areas with abundant wildlife or farms where the grass is long.

It is important to not squeeze a tick's body while it is eating. You could cause your dog to become irritated by the contents of its stomach and other innards. You should not pull too hard, as pulling can cause the head to be pulled under the skin of the dog. This can lead to infection if the head remains attached. If this happens, you should immediately seek medical attention.

Small hooks are available at pet shops that can be placed between the tick's body & your dog's skin to remove it safely.

You can find a lot of advice online about how to make ticks release their grip by lighting a cigarette.

You can either ask a friend or a vet to help you or view a YouTube video that explains how to remove ticks. The tick attaches to itself in a clockwise spiral. You can then use tweezers, or one of the hooks that are specially designed to grasp the tick's body, and gently twist it in an anticlockwise direction. This unhooks the tick, and prevents you from accidentally twisting its head.

It may seem odd to you that if the tick eventually falls off, why bother removing it? Lyme disease is a serious problem that ticks can carry in certain areas. This will require veterinary and medical attention. Lyme disease symptoms include fatigue, joint pain, and muscle pain. Lyme disease can also be transmitted to dogs by being bitten by a tick.

Mites

They are everywhere. Although they are generally harmless, some mites can be problematic for Thai Ridgeback dogs, especially the mange mite.

Mange mites can cause hair loss and itching by causing a hole in the skin. If left untreated, mange mites can cause permanent hair loss and damage to the dog's overall health.

Mange mites can severely affect the dog's immune system. The seemingly harmless mange infestation can be fatal if it is not treated.

Mange mites in dogs should be treated with conventional veterinary medicine. This condition is difficult to treat and can take a long time.

Itchy Thai Ridgebacks in autumn may have a reaction to harvest mites. This is especially true if your Thai Ridgeback lives on farmland. These mites can only cause irritation and can be removed with soap and water.

Ear Mites

Although ear mites are not visible to the naked eye, they can be easily seen with a microscope. These tiny mites can grow in dogs' ears and produce a brownish-colored discharge. Drops can be used to treat ear mites.

Flies

If your dog has open sores or wounds, flies can be a danger in summer. These big flies are constantly looking for places to lay eggs. They quickly turn into maggots and eat the flesh. This condition is known as "fly strike" and can often be found in pet rabbits or similar animals.

If your dog has any kind of anal or small wound, make sure that he is not exposed to this nasty parasite.

Other Common Illnesses

Every owner of a Thai Ridgeback should be aware that their dog's health is important. Dogs can get sick, sometimes they don't feel well for days and are more susceptible to getting sick than us.

This will allow you to be the best person to help your dog.

Diarrhea

Diarrhea can be a common problem and is not something to worry about. You can withhold food from the Thai Ridgeback for 24 hours and then slowly reintroduce it to him.

You should see your veterinarian immediately if you experience any of the following symptoms.

- It takes several days for the condition to resolve. The dog is shedding its blood
- Dog has eaten chocolate or artificial sweetener.
- The dog is either lethargic or stupefied Gums of the dog are either very pale or very deep red.

- If the neck of the dog is pinched, it does not return to its original position. This is an indication of dehydration.

Vomiting

Dogs will vomit out of choice. A single incident is not usually a problem.

For example, you might see your dog eating grass and then later notice their stomach contents and a pile of chewed grass. Even though dogs may not vomit from eating grass, it is possible that they do. Dogs may vomit when they feel sick and have to empty their stomach. This is similar to how we might need to vomit to feel better.

If the above circumstances lead to vomiting, the veterinarian should take the dog.

- The dog is not used to chewing bones or toys that might be stuck in his stomach.
- It is possible that the dog was exposed to poisons.
- Vomiting can cause obstruction of the dog's airway.
- You should consult your vet if any of the conditions listed above are causing you concern or seem to be too severe to ignore. You should consult your vet if any of these conditions are causing you concern or seem to be too severe.

Your dog knows you better than anyone. It is a good idea not to worry if you feel anxious. Your instincts may be a key factor in the health of your Thai Ridgeback dog.

Common Health Problems or Diseases

Congenital diseases can be passed from parent dogs to their puppies. This section will provide an overview of some common diseases that Thai Ridgebacks are susceptible to so that you can be prepared in case your Thai Ridgeback gets sick.

These diseases and disorders are common in the Thai Ridgeback breed:

- Atopic Dermatitis
- Epilepsy
- Entropion/Ectropion
- Gastric Torsion
- Hemangiosarcoma
- Hip Dysplasia
- Hypothyroidism
- Lymphoma
- Polymyositis
- Sebaceaous Adenitis

The following pages will provide an overview of the ten most common diseases, as well as information on their causes, symptoms, and treatment. You will be better prepared to deal with these diseases if they do occur. Your Thai Ridgeback's chances of a full recovery are greater if he is diagnosed early.

Atopic Dermatitis

Thai Ridgebacks simply call it atopic dermatitis. Your dog's skin condition is like a window into his inner health. Your dog's skin is a window into his inner health. The most common symptoms of skin allergies or other skin conditions include hair loss, scratching and frequent licking. You may also notice symptoms in your dog's internal system, such as vomiting or diarrhea due to allergies.

Dogs can become allergic to many things, including dust, pollen, mold, cigarettes, flea/flea products and perfumes. Your veterinarian might perform several diagnostic tests to diagnose skin allergies or other issues. To test for food allergies, your veterinarian will recommend switching to an allergen-free dog food for 10-12 weeks. Then, you can introduce possible allergens to see if your dog reacts. Once you've identified the source of the allergy, you can then take steps to eliminate it from your dog's diet.

Some allergies are not treatable by simply removing them completely from your dog's daily life. You cannot prevent your dog's exposure to pollen and dust. Some medications can help manage allergy symptoms in dogs. For example, Benadryl may be beneficial for some dogs. Supplements of fatty acids could also help improve your dog's skin or coat condition. A corticosteroid medication may be necessary if your dog has severe allergies. Your veterinarian should be closely monitoring these medications.

Allergies

Dog allergies can be very serious. Any dog can become allergic to dust, grains, or other substances in their environment.

Wheat Allergies

Grain allergy and wheat can lead to so many health issues that grain-free dog food is becoming a very common product. Many pet shops have at least one, if not more varieties.

What is wheat allergy? And what can it do to Thai Ridgeback dogs, Thai Ridgeback puppies and their pups? There are three types of wheat allergies in dogs. Each reaction has its own unique effects on the body and each one is equally harmful.

A dog can be allergic to wheat if it is fed a diet rich in wheat. Have a look.

- Itchy skin
- Open sores
- Ear infections
- Breathing problems
- Hives
- The sensation of burning in the throat or mouth
- Itchy and watery eyes
- Itchiness
- Dry skin
- Dandruff and poor coat condition
- Loose bowel movements
- Nasal congestion
- Rash
- Skin swelling
- Vomiting

Gluten sensitivity is a reaction to gluten. It can be found in wheat.

- Changes in behavior
- Bone and joint discomfort
- Pain
- Muscle cramps
- Weight loss
- Fatigue

In a very simple way, allergic reactions are caused by the dog's immune system.

Dogs that are allergic to a particular food must fight against the introduction of it into their bodies. The dog's immune system is affected and becomes less capable of coping with other illnesses and infections.

While wheat is the most common cause of dog food allergies, there are many other factors. The ingredients in dog food vary greatly depending on the brand, but they can contain bright colors (to appeal more to dog owners), unnatural flavors, and shocking chemical preservatives.

Look at your favorite dog food and browse the aisles at the pet shop. The composition of most dog food can be quite frightening. The long chemical names of dog food and the large number of them is alarming.

Epilepsy

Canine epilepsy, a serious condition that can affect Thai Ridgebacks, is well-known. This is the most common neurological condition in dogs, and can affect up to 5% of canine populations. Epilepsy is not a single condition. Epilepsy can be defined as any one of many conditions that are characterized by frequent seizures. Dogs can have seizures that are genetically inherited or may be caused by brain abnormalities. In some cases, they may also be due to an unknown cause.

Although there is an accepted classification system for seizures in humans, one has yet to be adopted for dogs. There are many types of seizures, including those that involve motor seizures or involuntary muscle movements. Automatism, a type motor seizure, often appears to be a voluntary behavior such as chewing or barking. Dogs can experience nonmotor seizures, but these are harder to spot because they usually involve the perception and activation of a sensory stimulus. The dog may be seen biting at nonexistent insects or staring into space.

There is no cure for epilepsy in canines, but there are many treatment options to manage the condition. To reduce seizures, anti-epileptic drugs such as potassium bromide and phenobarbital are often used. To improve treatment options, research is ongoing on the causes of canine epilepsy.

Entropion/Ectropion

Thai Ridgebacks can develop a variety of eye conditions, but the most common ones are entropion or ectropion. Entropion refers to a condition where a portion of the eyelid is inverted or folded. Ectropion is when the lower eyelid opens outwards, leaving the inner eyelid exposed. This can lead to irritation. Although ectropion is most common in Thai Ridgebacks, it can also occur due to hypothyroidism or facial nerve paralysis, scarring, chronic inflammation of the tissues around the eyes, and other conditions such as hypothyroidism. In many cases, ectropion can also be inherited. However, repeated eye infections and trauma to the eyes can lead to the development of the disease.

Entropion can be diagnosed easily because it causes irritation to the eye's surface and inflammation to surrounding tissues. Entropion is usually treated first by treating the secondary issues. For mild cases, lubrication may be done with artificial tears. Surgery may be necessary in severe or moderate cases to correct the malformation and prevent it from happening again. After surgery, follow-up care and medication may be necessary.

Ectropion can also be diagnosed by physical examination. However, additional blood and urine tests may need to be done to determine the root cause. Mild ectropion can be treated with medical therapy, such as lubricating drops for the eyes or ointments to stop the eye from drying. Surgery may be necessary in severe cases. Although the prognosis is generally good for surgical correction, some cases may require multiple surgeries to correct the problem permanently.

Gastric Torsion

Gastric torsion, also known as bloat or gastric torsion, is a common condition in large-breed dogs. However, it can also happen in Thai Ridgebacks. This happens when the dog's stomach expands and then rotates on its short axis. This can lead to serious conditions like pressure in the abdomen, distension of the stomach and damage to the heart. A decrease in perfusion could also happen, which can cause damage to the cells of the body and even organ failure.

Gastric torsion can cause anxiety, depression, stomach pain, diarrhea, vomiting, dry heaving, and excessive drooling. The dog might also feel a slower heartbeat, weaker pulse, and difficulty breathing as the condition progresses. Although the causes are not known, dogs who have had to deal with this disease in their past are more likely to develop it. Gastric torsion is also more common in deep-chested breeds.

Gastric torsion can rapidly escalate, resulting in emergency situations. It is important that you get treatment as soon as possible for your Thai Ridgeback. If your dog has cardiovascular symptoms, hospitalization is usually necessary. After the heart problem has been resolved, intubation will allow the pressure to be released from the abdomen. Surgery may then be required to correct the stomach's position. In some cases, additional treatments may be necessary to repair any organ damage.

Hemangiosarcoma

Hemangiosarcoma, a very aggressive and malignant type of tumor, affects the blood vessels which line the cells. Hemangiosarcoma tumors are most commonly found in the spleen. However, they can occur anywhere there is blood vessels. The liver, heart, bone and skin are all possible locations. Hemangiosarcoma tumors can be divided into three types: dermal, hypodermal, subcutaneous and visceral.

Hemangiosarcoma can cause a variety of symptoms, including visible bleeding, a lump under the skin and pale gums. Behavior changes such as weakness, depression, seizures, difficulty breathing, or unexplained weakness can also be caused by hemangiosarcoma. This condition affects the internal organs. Many dogs don't show any symptoms until their disease is severe.

Hemangiosarcoma can affect many breeds, but it is most common in dogs between 6 and 13 years old. A thorough examination and diagnostic tests such as blood counts, chemistry panels and x-rays will be required to diagnose hemangiosarcoma. A biopsy of the tumor is essential to confirm diagnosis. The location and size of the tumor will determine the treatment options. The best treatment options are available when the tumor is located under the skin. Many small dermal tumors can also be removed surgically. Radiation therapy and chemotherapy may be required for more severe tumors or those that affect the internal organs.

Hip Dysplasia

Hip dysplasia can be a musculoskeletal problem that affects many dogs, but is more common in larger and medium-sized breeds. This condition causes the hip joint to be malformed, which causes the femur and socket to pop out and cause pain and osteoarthritis. Although most dogs with this condition have normal hips, there are many factors that cause the soft tissue around the hip to develop in an abnormal manner. This can then lead to damage to the joint.

This condition can affect dogs of any age. Hip dysplasia can cause pain and discomfort in puppies as young as six months. These symptoms most often occur after and during exercise. The condition can become so severe that it makes daily activities difficult. The condition can progress to the point where the dog is unable to walk or become lame if the dog is not treated. Most cases of hip dysplasia don't manifest until the middle of life or later in life.

Hip dysplasia is a common condition in Thai Ridgebacks, and other breeds, that are closely related to arthritis symptoms. Many dogs will have an altered gait when walking or running. Some may resist moving that requires them fully to extend their back legs or flex their hips. Some dogs may walk with a bunny hop style and may struggle to navigate stairs. Hip dysplasia dogs can feel stiff and sore when they stand up or get up from a slumber. Dogs with this condition can become less energetic and lethargic over time.

Hip dysplasia is an inheritable condition. If your Thai Ridgeback has a genetic predisposition, you might not be able stop him from getting it. Some medical treatments, such as diet changes, anti-inflammatory medication, and supplements, may be able to help your dog manage the pain. They might also slow down the progression of the condition. Surgical treatments are the best and most effective treatment. The surgery can be used to align the bones and joints, or to replace the entire hip. It is possible to also remove the femoral heads and replace them with pseudo-joints. This is the most common surgical procedure.

Hypothyroidism

A deficiency of thyroid hormones is what causes this condition. The thyroid gland is an essential organ in the body that produces many hormones. These hormones play a key role in your dog's metabolism. Hypothyroidism is a condition where there is a decrease in the production of T3 or T4 hormones (liothyronine, levothyroxine). Hypothyroidism is more common in smaller and medium-sized dogs. Some breeds Hypothyroidism is most common Spayed/neutered dogs are more likely to be affected than intact dogs. are more susceptible than others. in dogs aged between 4-10 years.

Hypothyroidism can be characterized by lethargy and weakness, mental dullness as well as unexplained weight gain, hair fall, poor hair growth, scaling, frequent skin infections, intolerance of cold, seizures, and hair loss. Hypothyroidism may be caused by iodine deficiency or cancer. Sometimes, it can be a side effect of medical treatments such as surgery. It may take extensive testing to diagnose the condition and determine its cause and treatment plan.

Hypothyroidism is usually treated with medication and some type of diet modification. Other medications and synthetic hormones are used in medical treatments. Hypothyroidism can be treated with diet modifications, such as a low-fat diet during the initial phase. This condition is usually treated within a few weeks.

Lymphoma

Although lymphoma is rare in dogs, it can be seen in Thai Ridgebacks. Lymphoma is a form of cancer that develops in lymphocyte cells, which are part the immune system. Lymphocytes, a type white blood cell, are classified as T cells or B cells. The majority of lymphoma cases in dogs involve the B-lymphocytes.

There are many symptoms that can be associated with lymphoma, depending on how severe the condition is and where the tumor is located. The most common symptoms are loss of appetite, weight loss, weakness, and lethargy. It is difficult to diagnose lymphoma because the exact cause is not known. In addition to blood tests, urinalysis and an extensive examination, a thorough examination is required.

There is no cure for lymphoma. Many dogs will relapse after treatment. Radiation therapy and chemotherapy are the most common treatments. For cases involving dehydration, fluid therapy might be an option. There are some cases of lymphoma that never improve, and the goal of treatment in the majority of cases is to improve the dog's quality of life.

Polymyositis

Polymyositis, a form of immune-mediated disease that affects the skeletal muscles of dogs, is called "Polymyositis". Any type of skeletal muscle can be affected, including those in the limbs and the mouth. This condition can be a standalone or combined with immune-mediated diseases such as systemic Lupus.

The most common symptoms of this condition are stiffened gait and weight loss in middle-aged dogs. Polymyositis is most commonly seen in Thai Ridgebacks due to cancer, immune-mediated infection, or reaction to certain medications. A thorough medical history and examination will be required to diagnose the condition. In some cases, blood count, urine analysis and thoracic radiographs may also be necessary.

Corticosteroids are used to reduce the immune system's overreaction. This is the most common treatment for polymyositis. This is often the root cause of the condition. Sometimes, antibiotics are prescribed to fight infection. You may need to increase your pet's activity to build his muscles and prevent atrophy. Special feeding methods may be required for dogs with an enlarged stomach. Your veterinarian can tell you what type of food and how to feed your dog.

Sebaceaous Adenitis

Sebaceous adenitis, also known as inflammatory skin disorder in dogs, is a rare condition. The skin glands of middle-aged and young dogs are most commonly affected by this disease. Two types of sebaceous acne are present: one in long-coated dogs and the other in short coated. The Thai Ridgeback is most affected by the short-coated variety.

Sebaceous Adenitis is a condition that affects long-coated dogs. It can cause hair loss, severe itching, skin infections and skin lesions. Alopecia (often occurring in a circular pattern), mild skin scaling along the trunk and head, and secondary bacterial infections along hairline are common signs in short coated dogs. Researchers are still trying to determine the cause of this condition, but they have not yet found it.

Skin scrapings and endocrine functions tests are the most commonly used diagnostic methods for this condition. In certain cases, a skin biopsy and pathologic testing of the glands may be necessary. The severity of the condition and the type can vary. The most common treatments are to brush the skin to remove flaking, use antibacterial products and internal medication. You can also soak the skin in oil and massage it with various skin creams and oils to reduce itching.

Just like the neutering surgery, the spaying surgery also requires pre-surgical blood work to make sure your pup is healthy enough for this big surgery. Young and healthy dogs typically won't have any issues but it is still a good idea to get blood work done. Although spaying is a common surgery, it is still a fairly major one. Your veterinarian will give you specific instructions for post-surgery care and your dog will likely fully recover after a few weeks. Here are a few things to expect after your dog has the surgery:

- Some clinics will let you take home your pup after the surgery on the same day but other clinics may want her to stay overnight
- Pain medication will be prescribed on a need basis, most dogs don't need it but some do.
- Your dog may have some nausea in the first couple of days and may not be interested in food. This will go away after the first few days so no need to worry.
- Restrict her activity and play in the first week as excessive movement and exercise can cause swelling around her incision.
- Depending on what type of stitches your veterinarian used, they may need to be removed after a week. Your veterinarian will give you directions on how to check on the healing process of your dog's incision. Some modern-day stitches dissolve or fall out on their own.
- Make sure to keep her "cone of shame" on to prevent licking or nibbling of her incision.

If you notice any discharge around her incision, check in with your veterinarian to make sure everything is okay.

Your dog shouldn't be in excessive pain but if you notice that she is, let your veterinarian know as pain medication may be needed. Most dogs may feel lethargic and have low energy a few days after the surgery but don't worry. Give her a few days to recover before you get concerned.

Chapter Eight: Breeding Your Thai Ridgeback

Mating is a key part of the breeding process, and you should know all about it to grow and reach your goals as a breeder. When a dog gets the right age, it can, of course, bring forth puppies.

Mating Your Dam and Sire

Time has passed, and your dam and sire are now two-years-old and are ready to mate. All your hard work researching how to become a breeder, finding the right breeder to buy your male and female from as puppies, and all the care put forth raising them has culminated towards the end goal of mating. You now ask, what is next?

Once the bloody discharge begins to appear slightly pink and watery, usually one week into estrus, your female will start to ovulate, and she will show signs to start breeding. You will see indications of mating rituals. Your female will be amorous and dance around your male, have frequent urination around the yard to mark territory and begin to flag her tail to one side to allow your male to mount her. With increased hormonal activity, your male will also exhibit behaviors out of the ordinary during estrus, such as licking the female's urine, whining, howling, and he may urinate in the house to mark his territory.

Once the male mounts the female and he has entered her, the process known as a "tie" begins. The vagina will constrict around the shaft of the male's penis, and the male's penis, known as the bulbus glandis, swells inside the vagina holding the pair together for ten to twenty minutes while ejaculation takes place. The couple usually turns butt to butt, but sometimes they are side-by-side while they remain tied. Once a tie is evident, you should not intervene and try to break up mating; this will cause irreparable damage to both the male and female reproductive organs.

You should supervise the ties to keep your male and female calm; you want to be sure the female does not jerk quickly or twist suddenly and injure the penis.

Once the process is complete, they will separate on their own and will groom themselves. The process is exhausting for them, and they will drink plenty of water and sleep afterward. You need to keep an eye on the male to be sure his penis has retracted back inside his sheath like normal. You will find your male and female mating often during estrus; the sperm can last up to five days inside the female, and if you witness the first tie, you need to note the date on the calendar. Count out 63 days from the first tie, and that should be the day the puppies are born, called the "whelp date."

It is not easy to notice if your female is pregnant right away. For the first three weeks, you may not see any difference at all in her behavior. She may sleep a bit more, but other than that, the indications are slight. My female showed one subtle sign at the onset of pregnancy: her nipples began to grow ever so slightly and became pink. By the 3rd week, you will see more defined indications of pregnancy, such as increased appetite and thirst, and sleeping more. You will not begin to see an extended abdomen this early in the pregnancy.

After the 3rd week, you could go to the vet, have your female examined, and have an ultrasound performed to verify a successful mating; I always knew my female had a successful mating and did not have an ultrasound done.

Once the estrus cycle passed, and I witnessed a successful tie, I did begin to feed my female supplements to her diet, which included raw meat and raw eggs to give her extra protein. Some breeders recommend feeding the dam puppy food throughout the pregnancy to enhance nutrition. Your female will eat twice the amount of food she usually consumes while pregnant. Some females may have morning sickness and vomit intermittently during the first few weeks of pregnancy.

By mid-pregnancy, you will begin to see an enlarged abdomen and breast development. You may not notice milk production until the end of the gestation period, but you will notice the enlarged milking glands. The closer your female gets to the whelping date you will see her sleeping more, and she will exhibit nesting behavior. The term "nesting" refers to her seeking out corners of the house to hide. You may find her scratching at the carpet, digging holes in the yard, and other behaviors you have not seen before. This is an instinct to find a place to deliver her pups. Midway through her pregnancy, you should begin to gather the whelping supplies you need and build your whelping pen.

Once the whelping pen is built, you should encourage your female to nest in the pen so she feels familiar with the environment by the time the pups arrive. In the beginning, I sat in the whelping pen with my female and petted her so she became comfortable in the pen. By her second litter, she knew this was her zone and would go into the pen on her own to sleep.

Supplies

Whelping Pen Supplies

- **Whelping pen**: Plan for the pen to measure 9 feet long by 7 feet wide. The size may seem large, but when the pups grow, they will require this amount of space.
- **Whelping blankets**: it is best to have at least 4 to 6 blankets on hand. You will be laundering them regularly and will need a supply to keep in rotation. It is best to use twin-size blankets, not quilts as they do not launder well because of their bulkiness. Also, they do not launder to a sanitized acceptance. Wash the blankets with just a splash of bleach added to the detergent for maximum sanitization.
- **Heat lamps**: Two clamp lights with red 250-watt bulbs. The pups will require additional heat for the first 2 to 3 weeks. After that, they begin to generate their own heat, and you can remove the lamps. Pups need to remain between 85 and 90 degrees for the first five days of life.

- **Digital thermometer**: For use in determining when the pups are expected to arrive, the dam's temperature will drop down to about 98 degrees approximately 12-24 hours prior to whelping.
- **Free-standing thermometer**: To measure the temperature of the whelping pen during the puppies' first three weeks.
- **Digital scale**: To weigh each puppy.
- **Measuring tape**: To measure the length of each puppy.

Identification Supplies

- **Colored yarn**: Plan to have at least nine different colors of yarn to tie around the neck of each puppy for identification.
- **Litter collars**: can be found at pet stores and become handy once their new owners select the pups. Purchase multi-colored collars for identification, and get a pack of ten collars in the small adjustable size.

Cleaning Supplies

- **Six-month supply of newspapers**: Save the print sections, and not the advertisement and feature sections that are made of a non-absorbent paper. You will need this amount of paper for training the puppies to void upon once they begin to eat solid food.

- **Mop, bucket, broom, dustpan, and garbage bags**: You will need these items for proper sanitization of the whelping pen.
- **Gallon of bleach**: Bleach is the recommended product to use for its sanitizing properties. You only need two teaspoons of bleach per gallon of water to disinfect surfaces. Keep a fresh bucket of bleach water near the pen at all times. It is convenient to be on hand to mop unexpected clean-ups.
- **Latex gloves**: Two boxes of 100 gloves each should suffice.
- **Sanitizing gel**: For hand sanitization when handling the puppies.
- **Bathing basin**: In the beginning, you will be bathing the pups in the pen, and you will need a basin to wash them. I use a turkey roasting pan, and it works just fine. Once the pups get bigger, you can graduate them to the sink for daily baths.
- **Puppy shampoo**: For bathing when the pups are four weeks of age.
- **Nail clippers**: For use in keeping their razor-sharp nails clipped.

Feeding Supplies

- **Baby bottle**: A necessity if you must hand-feed any puppies.

- **Syringes**: In the event you need to hand-feed a pup and using a bottle is not effective. Wal-Mart offers these for free in the pharmacy. All you have to do is ask.

- **Nutritional supplement**: In the event you need to prepare formula for the pups, you must have the following ingredients on hand: 8-ounce container of vanilla yogurt, one can of evaporated milk (not low fat), two egg yolks, and infant vitamins.

- **Baby formula**: Buy one small container of powdered formula, which will be served as a nutritional supplement during the third week.

- **Rice cereal**: One box of baby food will be the introduction to solid food.

- **Puppy food**: Plan on 50 pounds of dry premium puppy food for starters.

- **Milk Bones@ biscuits**: Have a box of small Milk Bones@ on hand; as the pups grow, they enjoy them as a treat.

- **Litter-feeding bowl**: Specifically designed stainless steel bowl for feeding a litter of pups. This can be found in pet stores.

- **Large water bowl**: As the pups grow, they will drink a lot of water and need a large stainless-steel bowl.

Medical Supplies

- **Hemostats:** For clamping umbilical cords before cutting the cord in the event the mother is unable to perform the task.
- **Children's scissors**: To cut the umbilical cord after clamping.
- **Infant nasal aspirator**: For removing amniotic fluid from the puppies' nose and throat if the dam is unable to do this.
- **KY Jelly**: To lubricate the thermometer for rectal temperature readings and for use when assisting with the delivery process.
- **Rubbing alcohol**: To sanitize supplies.
- **Phone numbers**: Have your veterinarian's phone number readily available in the event of an emergency. If the office does not provide 24-hour services, then also include an emergency veterinarian's phone number if your emergency falls outside regular office hours.

Toys

Have soft, plush toys on hand for when the pups grow. Avoid toys with any removable parts such as eyes, noses, and squeakers, so the pups do not choke. Plush toys should be laundered often. Other toys can include balls, ropes, and the best toy of all is an empty water bottle with the cap and label removed; the pups go crazy for such a simple item.

Camera

If you do not own a digital camera, you should consider getting one. You will want to document the journey from birth through adoption of your puppies by taking daily pictures and videos. Uploading your pictures and videos online offers prospective new owners of your puppies' valuable insight on the growth, development, and care your puppies receive.

Stages of Labor

The Onset of Labor:

Pregnancy in dogs lasts approximately 62 to 64 days. One week before the due date, begin to take the dam's rectal temperature daily. Lubricate with KY jelly, insert the thermometer about an inch into the rectum, and wait for the reading. Her temperature should be between 101º and 102.5º Fahrenheit. When the pet's temperature drops below 100º F, she should deliver the pups within twenty-four hours. A week before whelping, give your female a bath. If you have a long hair female, trim the hair around the vulva and nipples.

Stage One of Labor:

During this stage, the cervix begins to dilate, and uterine contractions begin. These contractions are painful. She will appear uncomfortable, restless, and may pace and pant. She probably will not eat, and she may vomit. This is the longest stage of labor. It generally lasts six to eighteen hours. By the end of this period, the cervix will have completely dilated for the puppies to pass. During this time, keep the mother's environment quiet and calm

Stage Two of Labor:

Plan to stay with the dam for the duration of delivery. During this stage, uterine contractions become stronger. The placental water sack breaks, and a light-colored fluid passes. Placentas are expelled after each puppy arrives. The average litter size for Thai Ridgeback is five puppies, and they usually appear every half-hour to an hour after the first one is delivered. As each one arrives, the mother will instinctively tear away the sac, which is called the "amniotic membrane," chew off the umbilical cord, lick the puppy clean, and stimulate the puppy to breathe. It is essential to let the mother do this because it is the beginning of the bonding process. The mother will eat the afterbirths. If she does not tear away the sac and lick the pups to stimulate respiration, you should help tear the sack open, clear all fluids away from the pup's nose and mouth using the infant nasal aspirator, and gently rub the puppy on its chest to stimulate breathing. You may need to assist with cutting the umbilical cord using the children's scissors in your supply kit. You may have to assist with helping a puppy through the birth canal by very gently pulling in a downward motion. You should keep a bowl of water in the whelping pen for the exhausted mother to drink. Bring the dish to her, and take it away when she is done.

Stage Three of Labor:

When all the puppies have been born, the female enters this 3rd stage of labor, during which time the uterus contracts fully, expelling any remaining blood, placenta, and fluid. You know all the puppies have been delivered with this indicator. The mother will eat everything she had expelled, which helps to stimulate milk production.

Post Labor:

At this point, the mother is exhausted. She will need to relieve herself and want to stretch. Give her a few minutes to go outside, walk around the yard, get a drink of water, and perhaps get something to eat. I always reward my female with praise and a few bites of raw chicken. She is usually not hungry for a few hours after delivering her puppies but does need steady nourishment, and I continue to offer her bites of food until she goes to her food bowl on her own. While she is away from her puppies, you should change the soiled blankets with clean blankets and mop up areas that may be unsanitary. I use this time to clean my female up a bit before she goes back to nurse her puppies.

The newborns do not generate their own heat and can develop life-threatening hypothermia during the first weeks of life. The puppies begin to generate their own heat and develop the shiver reflex at around three weeks of age.

Turn on both of the heat lamps to warm the whelping pen and avoid drafts near there. Place the free-standing thermometer on the floor of the pen near the puppies and maintain a temperature between 85 ° and 90 ° for the next seven days.

During the second week, maintain the temperature between 80 °and 85 °. During the third week, keep the temperature between 75 ° and 80 °. The temperature during the fourth through eighth week should remain between 70 ° and 75 °. The heat lamps should be placed 4′ to 5′ above the puppies so you gently warm them.

Identify each puppy right away by tying a piece of different colored yarn around the neck of each puppy. Document the length and weight of each puppy. To easily weigh the puppies line a small container (such as a food storage container) with a washcloth. Place the container on the digital scale and weigh.

Now place a puppy into the container to weigh. Deduct for the weight of the empty container, and you will have the accurate weight of the puppy. Continue to document the length and weight of each puppy daily for the next two weeks. This will give you a good indication that the puppies are growing correctly and receiving enough nourishment. On average, a puppy will double its weight by one-week-old followed by a consistent 5% to 10% increase daily. Next, you will need to identify the gender of each puppy. The female puppy will have a tiny leaf-like shape between her back legs near the anus; this is the vagina. The male puppy will have a tiny dot near the belly; this is the penis.

The day after whelping you could take your dam to the vet to get a post-partum check-up. Your veterinarian will feel her uterus to make sure all the pups and placentas have been expelled, as well as give her on an antibiotic to prevent an infection from taking hold.

Weeks One Through Eight

This section will provide guidance on what to expect in the first eight weeks of your puppy's life, regardless of whether you are caring for a single puppy or a whole litter.

Because puppies are born with their eyes and ears closed, they rely entirely on their mother and you for protection and help. Even though they won't be able move much, it is important to take the necessary steps to puppy proof the area where your puppies are being raised.

If the mother dog is present, ensure that her water dish is high enough to prevent a puppy from drowning. Children under the age of 3 should be supervised and supervised at all times.

Weight gain is an important part of a puppy's development. Make sure that every puppy gets the same opportunity to nurse from its mother. If a puppy's weight gains are slow, it may not be getting enough nursing opportunities from its mother.

The puppies will start to be more active within the first few days of their birth and will soon be able use their senses of small to explore the surrounding area. Although their eyes and ears are still closed, they will be more mobile. To reduce injury to themselves or others, you'll need to trim their nails. You can set aside time each week for them to trim their nails.

Their eyes will open during week two and they will be capable of hearing sounds. The puppies will actively explore their environment with their new senses. It is important to keep their space free from potential dangers.

Some puppies might be able to urinate on their own. If this is the case, clean up any waste. If they are not responding to the warm washcloth, you can continue to massage their bottoms with the warm towel if you are hand-raising. The puppies will still need to be nursed, but less often.

The puppies may have grown out of their whelping boxes by weeks three or four. To help them get out and stretch their legs, line an area outside the box with newspaper. However, make sure they are supervised when they are not in the box. The puppies can then be given semi-solid food and water at the end of the week.

The puppies can still be nursed by their mother during weeks five and six, even though they have been introduced to solid food. Hand-raising the puppies requires that you feed them less milk substitute and promote solid food. You can begin housetraining the puppies in week six by taking them outside as soon as they have finished eating.

If puppies are being raised solely by their mothers, then week seven should be the time they start to wean. At this stage, puppies that have been raised by their mother should not be fed bottle-fed. Puppy's eight-week-old age will allow them to be vaccinated and have a physical exam.

Post Delivery

Some issues can arise weeks or days after your dog's birth. You should contact your veterinarian if you see any symptoms similar to the ones listed below. It is easier to treat a problem if symptoms are detected quickly.

Post Delivery Fever

Mothers may experience a fever a few days after giving birth to their litter. This is normal, unless there is vomiting, weakness of the muscles, or any other symptoms.

Metritis

Metritis refers to inflammation of the uterus or uterine tissues due to a bacterial infection. Symptoms may appear within 24 to 48 hours of delivery. They can include anxiety, fever, vomiting, nausea, vomiting, neglect of dogs, unusually colored or sour vaginal discharge, and lack of appetite. This condition can be treated with antibiotics.

Hemorrhage

Although spotting and small amounts of blood after delivery are normal, heavy vaginal blood flow is dangerous. Seek emergency medical help immediately.

Mastitis

Mastitis refers to inflammation of the breasts or breast/mammary tissues due to bacterial infection in mammary ducts. Your dog might try to stop your puppy from nursing, as it can cause her pain. The puppies may become starved. There may not be any other symptoms, aside from reddening nipples. It is important to examine your dog's nipples every day and keep track of her weight to determine if she has mastitis.

The reason puppies aren't gaining weight is that they aren't being allowed to get enough nursing. If the dog is suffering from mastitis, it should be brought to the vet.

If mastitis progresses, the milk could change from a white color to a yellowish green. The milk may show signs of bleeding or if the nipple has been blotted on a tissue. A fever may be experienced by the mother dog. The infected area may become a pustule or abscessed in severe cases. The affected tissue may turn dark brown or black. The dead tissue should be removed surgically when this happens.

Eclampsia

Hypocalcemia (low calcium levels in canines) is the cause of eclampsia. This happens when a mother dog received calcium supplements or was not properly nourished during her pregnancy. This is more common in dogs who were not fed regularly and stray pregnant dogs.

After two weeks of nursing, symptoms may begin to manifest. They could include restlessness and neglect of puppies as well as inability to walk or move smoothly. If she is not treated, she may lose her ability of standing and could even have seizures. Eclampsia can be easily treated by intravenous calcium therapy, administered by a veterinarian.

How to Properly Handle a Newborn Puppy

Properly holding a puppy in your arms is crucial for his health and safety. You should not handle puppies for the first three weeks, as they may not be able to hear or see. Talk to the mother if you are present. Slowly approach the whelping container while speaking calmly to her. If the puppy becomes anxious or growls at you, please leave it alone. She is entitled to protect her litter. Because the puppies are so close, she may warn them against pinning them. This could make them distrust you and become more anxious as they get older.

Start by touching a puppy's skin with your fingertips, if your dog is willing to let you approach them. This is a way to introduce yourself to your dog and let him know you don't mean any harm. Place your hands underneath the belly of the puppy and gently lift it up. Make sure to support his head and tuck his legs under his back. If his legs hang down in midair, the puppy might panic. He will feel more secure if his legs are close to his body. If you are hand-raising, take care of the puppy and then return him to his mother.

Although touch is a critical part of socialization, it can also have a negative effect on a puppy's health and behavioral development. It can lead to death if a puppy is dropped or squeezed too tightly. A child should not be allowed to handle a puppy under three weeks of age. You can hold the puppy and allow a child to touch him.

You can allow your puppy to be held if he is at least eighteen months old and has his eyes open. Explain to the puppy that puppies are fragile and must be handled with care. Transfer the puppy to you by placing him on a table or in a chair. Unsupervised play with a puppy is not allowed. While a puppy can be played with at times, it is best to keep it from being left unsupervised.

How to Care for Weak Newborns

For the first few weeks after their birth, all puppies must be dependent on you or their mother. Some puppies require extra care to thrive, such as being fed, cleaned, stimulated and encouraged to excrete waste.

To take his first breath, a puppy must be stimulated when he enters the world through the birth canal. It may be as simple as removing gestational fluid from the airway with an aspirator, and then rubbing it with a towel.

Even after several minutes of stimulation, your puppy might not be breathing. Don't assume the worst and abandon your puppy. There are many ways you can revive a dog. You can start by doing rescue breathing. As you would with a person, place the dog on its back and gently inhale into his mouth.

You should not take in a full lung! Your lung capacity is much greater than that of a puppy. This can cause irreversible damage in his lungs. Instead, imagine that you are consuming hot soup. Press down on his chest with your fingertips and then continue to massage his body using the towel.

A shock to the system is necessary for some methods of revival. You can use an eyedropper, or the tip of your finger to apply brandy to the puppy's tongue. Some breeders will allow their puppy to be bathed in hot and cold water.

A sudden change in the water temperature can cause the puppy to take a deep breath. Pay close attention to when your puppy starts breathing. Wrap him in a towel immediately and dry him. This method should not be used if you don't have hot water. Scalding sensitive skin of a puppy is not a good idea.

Some puppies won't take their first breath. There are other things that must be done. After your dog gives birth, wrap the body in a towel. You can then contact your veterinarian to ask how to respect the remains.

Even if there are no mishaps, puppies born to healthy parents are still at risk for what is called fading puppy syndrome. Although the syndrome is not a specific disease, it can be used to describe a range of symptoms that could have multiple causes. The health of puppies can change from being healthy to becoming unhealthy. Puppies may lose interest and stop nursing. They might also lose weight, feel lethargic or cry out in pain. The symptoms may manifest as soon as 48 hours after birth, but may not appear for up to 3 weeks depending on the cause. This can be either a genetic defect or a bacterial infection.

You should first check that your puppy is getting enough time with his mother to nurse and is well hydrated. You can also give him a bottle if you are able. Contact a veterinarian if his condition doesn't improve or worsen. Although there are no cures for genetic defects, the puppy is likely to die. However, it is important to take bacterial and viral infections seriously. Because the puppies live in close proximity to their mother and each other, it is possible for a virus to be transmitted easily and infect the whole litter. The health of the litter is ensured by treating an ill puppy promptly.

Nursing with a Mother Dog

After all puppies have been born, they should start nursing within 24 hours. This will allow them to receive their mother's colostrum rich in antibodies. These antibodies will keep them healthy until they are vaccinated.

For up to four weeks, puppies will be nursed by their mothers until they can eat solid food. They will start nursing approximately every two hours in the beginning. The mother will then lick the bottoms of her baby to remove any waste. After that, they will fall asleep until it is time for them to nurse again.

A puppy can nurse from his mother, and he can even stop at any time to start his own feedings, provided that the mother has enough milk. This eliminates the possibility of a puppy being fed too much or too little.

Sometimes, a puppy might not be able to reach his nipple or may be prevented from nursing by his mother. This behavior can be caused by many factors. This could be due to a genetic defect in the puppy or the mother. However, a pregnant woman may reject the majority of her litter if she has an illness. You should carefully examine a puppy who is not being fed. If your puppy appears to be healthy, you can attach him to one the mother's nipples. To avoid disturbing the mother as she is near the litter, it's best to do this with another person. Call your veterinarian if the same puppy keeps being rejected, or if the mother is rejecting other puppies. You will need to bottle-feed the puppies that are rejected with milk substitute while you wait.

Monitoring a puppy's weight can help you determine if it is nursing properly. The puppies should gain weight steadily for the first week after birth. To determine if puppies are getting enough food, the first week is a good time to check their weight.

A puppy that is too small should be allowed to rest with his mother. The breed of dog will determine how much a puppy should weigh every week. Your veterinarian can give you an exact estimate of the weight of your puppies after one week.

Your dog will need to be fed while she's nursing her litter. Your dog was eating twice as much puppy food at the end of her gestation than she would have before pregnancy. Puppy food is specially formulated to meet the nutritional needs of puppies. Keep her on the puppy food five to six times per day. You can give her a bowl of food to eat whenever she feels hungry.

You can also leave water for your puppy so that she is hydrated. You must ensure that any bowls are not placed in the box.

Conclusion

The Thai Ridgeback is a pet that is both strong and sweet. He loves his family and is very loyal that he would protect them no matter what. He's also intelligent and wiling to please but because of his hunter instincts, he has a tendency to be independent, stubborn and have a strong prey drive.

He is averagely healthy and when it comes to grooming, he is pretty much low-maintenance. His exercise needs aren't low though. He needs everyday walks or runs for around an hour.

Keep in mind that whatever probable problem behaviors that your ridgeback may possess, can be reduced by correct training, consistency, patience, and right treatment. We hope that this guide has given you useful information about the Thai Ridgeback.

Everything now depends on you so, all the best!

Glossary of Terms

Adoption – A process in which a rescued pet is placed into a permanent home.

Acute Disease – refers to a disease or illness that manifests quickly

Agility – This is a sport in which the dog handler guides and instructs the dog through a course of obstacles while being timed. Accuracy through this obstacle course is paramount. The dogs must complete the obstacle course without a leash or toys (or food) as incentives. The handler can only use voice, movement and various body signals in order to direct the dog.

AKC – American Kennel Club, the largest purebred dog registry in the United States

Almond Eye – Referring to an elongated eye shape rather than a rounded shape

Apple Head – A round-shaped skull

Balance – A show term referring to all of the parts of the dog, both moving and standing, which produce a harmonious image

Beard – Long, thick hair on the dog's underjaw

Best in Show – An award given to the only undefeated dog left standing at the end of judging

Bitch – A female dog

Bite – The position of the upper and lower teeth when the dog's jaws are closed; positions include level, undershot, scissors, or overshot

Blaze – A white stripe running down the center of the face between the eyes

Board – To house, feed, and care for a dog for a fee

Breed – A domestic race of dogs having a common gene pool and characterized appearance/function

Breed Standard – A published document describing the look, movement, and behavior of the perfect specimen of a particular breed

Buff – An off-white to gold coloring

Canine- a term for dog.

Canine Teeth- also known as eye teeth, the largest teeth found in the dog's mouth. They are long, curved teeth on either side of the mouth, top and bottom.

Chronic Disease – refers to a disease that will last indefinitely.

Clip – A method of trimming the coat in some breeds

Coat – The hair covering of a dog; some breeds have two coats, and outer coat and undercoat; also known as a double coat. Examples of breeds with double coats include Shiba Inu, German Shepherd, Siberian Husky, Akita, etc.

Condition – The health of the dog as shown by its skin, coat, behavior, and general appearance

Crate – A container used to house and transport dogs; also called a cage or kennel

Crossbreed (Hybrid) – A dog having a sire and dam of two different breeds; cannot be registered with the AKC

Dam (bitch) – The female parent of a dog;

Dock – To shorten the tail of a dog by surgically removing the end part of the tail.

Double Coat – Having an outer weather-resistant coat and a soft, waterproof coat for warmth; see above.

Drop Ear – An ear in which the tip of the ear folds over and hangs down; not prick or erect

Entropion – A genetic disorder resulting in the upper or lower eyelid turning in

Fancier – A person who is especially interested in a particular breed or dog sport

Fawn – A red-yellow hue of brown

Feathering – A long fringe of hair on the ears, tail, legs, or body of a dog

Groom – To brush, trim, comb or otherwise make a dog's coat neat in appearance

Heel – To command a dog to stay close by its owner's side

Hip Dysplasia – A condition characterized by the abnormal formation of the hip joint

Inbreeding – The breeding of two closely related dogs of one breed

Kennel – A building or enclosure where dogs are kept

Litter – A group of puppies born at one time

Markings – A contrasting color or pattern on a dog's coat

Mask – Dark shading on the dog's foreface

Mate – To breed a dog and a bitch

Neuter – To castrate a male dog or spay a female dog

Pads – The tough, shock-absorbent skin on the bottom of a dog's foot

Parti-Color – A coloration of a dog's coat consisting of two or more definite, well-broken colors; one of the colors must be white

Pedigree – The written record of a dog's genealogy going back three generations or more

Pied – A coloration on a dog consisting of patches of white and another color

Prick Ear – Ear that is carried erect, usually pointed at the tip of the ear

Puppy – A dog under 12 months of age

Purebred – A dog whose sire and dam belong to the same breed and who are of unmixed descent

Saddle – Colored markings in the shape of a saddle over the back; colors may vary

Shedding – The natural process whereby old hair falls off the dog's body as it is replaced by new hair growth.

Sire – The male parent of a dog

Smooth Coat – Short hair that is close-lying

Spay – The surgery to remove a female dog's ovaries, rendering her incapable of breeding

Trim – To groom a dog's coat by plucking or clipping

Undercoat – The soft, short coat typically concealed by a longer outer coat

Vaccine – a shot that is given to a dog to help produce immunity to a specific disease.

Wean – The process through which puppies transition from subsisting on their mother's milk to eating solid food

Whelping – The act of birthing a litter of puppies

Index

Index

Index

Index

I

L

M

N

Index

O

P

R

Index

Index

U

V

W

Index

Photo Credits

Page 3, Svetography via Canva.com (Canva Pro License)

https://www.canva.com/photos/MADFUFS1eTg-thai-ridgeback-puppy/

Page 6, Ksenia Raykova via Canva.com (Canva Pro License)

https://www.canva.com/photos/MADs1r0bk2E-thai-ridgeback-puppy-posing-indoors-by-leaning-on-owner-hands/

Page 15, Svetography via Canva.com (Canva Pro License)

https://www.canva.com/photos/MADFE_gyvVY-thai-ridgeback-puppy-isolated-on-white/

Page 35, Mindaugas Dulinskas via Canva.com (Canva Pro License)

https://www.canva.com/photos/MAEZz1ySnwI-thai-ridgeback-face/

References

American Kennel Club n.d, accessed 10 September 2021, https://www.akc.org/dog-breeds/thai-ridgeback/

Amy Tokic 2013, PetGuide.com accessed 17 September 2021, https://www.petguide.com/breeds/dog/thai-ridgeback/#:~:text=An%20athletic%20and%20high%2Denergy,gum%20infections%20and%20bad%20breath.

Animal Care Tips 2010, accessed 8 September 2021, https://animalcaretip.com/how-to-care-for-your-thai-ridgeback/

AZ Animals 2022, accessed 12 September 2021, https://a-z-animals.com/animals/thai-ridgeback/

Calvin L. n.d, Dogtemperament.com, accessed 23 September 2021, https://dogtemperament.com/thai-ridgeback-temperament/

Daily Paws n.d, accessed 21 September 2021, https://www.dailypaws.com/dogs-puppies/dog-breeds/thai-ridgeback

Dog Breed Info n.d, accessed 11 September 2021, https://www.dogbreedinfo.com/thairidgeback.htm

Dogbreedslist.info n.d, accessed 8 September 2021, https://www.dogbreedslist.info/all-dog-breeds/thai-ridgeback.html

References

Dogell n.d, accessed 17 September 2021, https://dogell.com/en/dog-breed/thai-ridgeback

Dogtime.com n.d, accessed 12 September 2021, https://dogtime.com/dog-breeds/thai-ridgeback#/slide/1

Dog-Learn n.d, accessed 15 September 2021, https://www.dog-learn.com/dog-breeds/thai-ridgeback/care

Dr Linda Simon n.d, Dogzone.com, accessed 10 September 2021, https://www.dogzone.com/breeds/thai-ridgeback/

Embrace Pet Insurance n.d, accessed 22 September 2021, https://www.embracepetinsurance.com/dog-breeds/thai-ridgeback

Hundeo n.d, accessed 8 September 2021, https://www.hundeo.com/en/dog-breeds/thai-ridgeback/

Jenna Stregowski 2022, The Spruce Pets, accessed 13 September 2021, https://www.thesprucepets.com/thai-ridgeback-breed-profile-5079573

Melissa Smith 2016, Playful, accessed 8 September 2021, https://www.petful.com/breeds/thai-ridgebacks/

Midway Animal Hospital n.d, accessed 22 September 2021, https://midwayanimal.com/client-resources/breed-info/thai-ridgeback/

Nicole Cosgrove 2022, Hepper, accessed 7 September 2021, https://www.hepper.com/thai-ridgeback/

References

PawDiet n.d, accessed 10 September 2021, https://www.pawdiet.com/breeds/best-dog-food-for-thai-ridgeback/

Petfinder.com n.d, accessed 8 September 2021, https://www.petfinder.com/dog-breeds/thai-ridgeback/

Pet ID Register n.d, accessed 10 September 2021, https://petidregister.com/thai-ridgeback/do-thai-ridgeback-need-to-be-groomed-regularly/

PetMD n.d, accessed 26 September 2021, https://www.petmd.com/dog/breeds/c_dg_thai_ridgeback

Pet Net ID n.d, accessed 7 September 2021, https://petnetid.com/breed/thai-ridgeback/thai-ridgeback-grooming-brush-kit-price/

Royal Canin n.d, accessed 12 September 2021, https://www.royalcanin.com/my/dogs/breeds/breed-library/thai-ridgeback-dog

United Kennel Club n.d, accessed 9 September 2021, https://www.ukcdogs.com/thai-ridgeback

Vetstreet.com n.d,, accessed 18 September 2021, http://www.vetstreet.com/dogs/thai-ridgeback

Wag Labs n.d, accessed 26 September 2021, https://wagwalking.com/activity/activities-for-thai-ridgebacks

References

Wisdom Panel n.d, accessed 8 September
2021, https://www.wisdompanel.com/en-us/dog-breeds/thai-ridgeback

www.ingramcontent.com/pod-product-compliance
Lightning Source LLC
Chambersburg PA
CBHW071420090426
42737CB00011B/1525